Richard Marsden

# ESSENTIALS

GCSE German

evision Guide

# Contents

# Contents

## Leisure and Free Time

## Widening Horizons

# Exam Overview

## Listening

You usually have five minutes to look through the exam paper before the test starts. Use this time sensibly by checking what topics have come up and then making notes on the paper to help you.

The following are some points to remember:

- Read each question carefully. Sometimes a single word can make a big difference to the meaning. For example, the questions, 'What subjects does he like?' and 'What subjects does he dislike?' require very different answers.
- Some of the questions may be in German, so make sure you know the different 'question words'. For example, don't mix up wo? and wer? (where? and who?).
- Don't panic if you're unable to answer the question the first time you hear the recording. Remember, you'll hear the recordings twice.
- You aren't expected to understand everything that you hear in the recording. You may just need to work out the gist of what's being said.
- Never leave a blank space because this will always score zero. So, if you're genuinely stuck, try to make a sensible guess.

- Listen carefully for little words that can reverse the meaning of what you hear: nicht (*not*) is an obvious example, but kaum (*hardly*), nie (*never*) and selten (*rarely*) can also be tricky.
- Don't assume that the first phrase you hear is the correct one; listen to the question carefully. For example, if you hear, 'Ich fahre selten mit dem Auto in die Stadtmitte, ich fahre oft mit dem Bus' and the question asks how the person gets to school, the answer will not be 'by car', even though you hear the phrase mit dem Auto.

## Reading

As with the listening part of the exam, having a good knowledge of vocabulary is essential for the reading section. In fact, it is even more important in reading because the examiner will expect you to be able to deal with some unfamiliar words by using communication strategies to work out the meaning. For example, if you know that spielen means 'to play', you'll be expected to know that ein Spieler means 'a player' and that ein Spiel is 'a game'.

- Watch out for tenses: you have to show that you understand the different tenses in order to obtain grade C or above. Make sure you know how to distinguish them. For example, don't mix up the future (Ich werde… *I will…*) with the conditional (Ich würde… *I would…*).
- Some high frequency words, such as oft, immer, nie, außer and immer noch can alter the meaning of a sentence. Make sure you read each sentence carefully.
- In questions aimed at the highest grades, you may have to come to conclusions or draw inferences from

what you read. For example, if you read: 'Er macht nicht immer seine Hausaufgaben, er findet Mathe schwer und er versteht sich nicht gut mit seinen Lehrern' you can conclude that this person is probably having problems at school.

- When revising, try to learn vocabulary in categories so that you can see the connections between words. If the answer to a question about a person's favourite hobby is 'reading', the word lesen may not even be there at all. Words such as ein Roman (a novel) or eine Zeitung (newspaper) might give you the answer instead.

## Speaking

The speaking exam is part of the controlled assessment. You'll have to produce two pieces of spoken assessment during the GCSE course, which will be marked by your German teacher. Each assessment should be between four and six minutes long.

Your teacher can help you to plan what you want to talk about. You're allowed notes with you when you do the test, but these can't be more than 30–40 words. You can devise your own task or use one provided by the exam board. Check with your teacher about what exactly is allowed.

- Be aware that at some point in the test your teacher may ask you a question that you haven't prepared an answer for.
- Make sure that what you intend to say contains plenty of opinions and reasons to make it more personal.
- Try to cover a variety of time frames, for example, saying what you've done recently to illustrate your point.
- When revising, see if you can ask someone to record some key phrases for you. You will pick up extra marks if you can pronounce 'ch', 's', and 'z' in an authentic German way, so practise saying words out loud that contain these sounds. Remember also to pronounce vowels with an Umlaut correctly, i.e. ä, ö, and ü.

- Avoid answers that are too short – always try to develop what you say. But, don't try to give overlong answers that sound like pre-rehearsed presentations. You may lose marks if your conversation sounds more like a recitation.
- Try to include some longer sentences by using connectives, such as weil, obwohl and sobald, or by using *relative pronouns*.

## Writing

The writing exam is part of the controlled assessment. You'll have to produce two pieces of written work during the GCSE course. You will do this written work in school and it will be marked by the exam board.

To gain the very highest marks these two pieces should come to about 600 words overall.

You can do a task devised by the exam board, by your teacher or by yourself. Check with your teacher that your choice of topic is suitable. You can produce a draft and ask your teacher to comment on it using an official feedback form.

- You should include opinions, reasons and justifications wherever possible and use a variety of tenses.
- You're allowed to use a dictionary when writing the final version of your work under supervision. Try to use the dictionary only to check spellings and genders. Avoid

the temptation to look up new words that you don't know as this can lead to misunderstandings and errors.
- You need to include as much complexity as possible in your work, i.e. longer sentences, complex grammatical structures and a variety of interesting vocabulary.
- Make use of adverbs, adjectives and pronouns where you can.

# Essential German

## Numbers

| | | | | | | |
|---|---|---|---|---|---|---|
| 0 | null | 20 | zwanzig | first | **der / die / das erste** |
| 1 | eins | 21 | einundzwanzig | second | **der / die / das zweite** |
| 2 | zwei | 22 | zweiundzwanzig | third | **der / die / das dritte** |
| 3 | drei | 23 | dreiundzwanzig | fourth | **der / die / das vierte** |
| 4 | vier | 30 | dreißig | twentieth | **der / die / das zwanzigste** |
| 5 | fünf | 31 | einunddreißig | thirtieth | **der / die / das dreißigste** |
| 6 | sechs | 35 | fünfunddreißig | | |
| 7 | sieben | 40 | vierzig | | |
| 8 | acht | 50 | fünfzig | | |
| 9 | neun | 60 | sechzig | | |
| 10 | zehn | 70 | siebzig | | |
| 11 | elf | 80 | achtzig | | |
| 12 | zwölf | 90 | neunzig | | |
| 13 | dreizehn | 100 | hundert | | |
| 14 | vierzehn | 101 | hunderteins | | |
| 15 | fünfzehn | 1000 | tausend | | |
| 16 | sechzehn | | | | |
| 17 | siebzehn | about 10 | ungefähr zehn | | |
| 18 | achtzehn | about 20 | ungefähr zwanzig | | |
| 19 | neunzehn | | | | |

## Months

| | | | | | | | |
|---|---|---|---|---|---|---|---|
| **Januar** | January | **Mai** | May | **September** | September |
| **Februar** | February | **Juni** | June | **Oktober** | October |
| **März** | March | **Juli** | July | **November** | November |
| **April** | April | **August** | August | **Dezember** | December |

## Days and Dates

| | |
|---|---|
| **Montag** | Monday |
| **Dienstag** | Tuesday |
| **Mittwoch** | Wednesday |
| **Donnerstag** | Thursday |
| **Freitag** | Friday |
| **Samstag /** | |
| **Sonnabend** | Saturday |
| **Sonntag** | Sunday |

**Den Wievielten haben wir heute?**
What is the date today?

**Heute ist der zwölfte Juli.**
Today is the 12th July.

**Heute ist der dreißigste Oktober.**
Today is the 30th October.

## The Time

| Wie spät ist es? / Wieviel Uhr ist es? What time is it? | Es ist... | It is... |
|---|---|---|
| | ein Uhr | 1 o'clock |
| | zwei Uhr | 2 o'clock |
| | sechs Uhr | 6 o'clock |
| | ein Uhr zehn | ten past one |
| | ein Uhr zwanzig | twenty past one |
| | zwei Uhr dreißig | |
| | (or **halb** drei) | two thirty |
| | vier Uhr fünfzehn | |
| | (or **Viertel nach vier**) | four fifteen |
| | sechs Uhr fünfundvierzig | |
| | (or **Viertel vor** sieben) | six forty-five |

| | |
|---|---|
| **um** | at |
| **gegen** | around |
| **um achtzehn Uhr** | at 6pm |
| **gegen zwanzig Uhr** | around 8pm |
| **Mitternacht** | midnight |
| **Mittag** | midday |
| **eine Minute** | minute |
| **eine Sekunde** | second |

German speakers often use the 24-hour clock. Don't be caught out!

## Colours

| rot | red | orange | orange |
|---|---|---|---|
| blau | blue | braun | brown |
| grün | green | rosa | pink |
| gelb | yellow | lila | purple |
| weiß | white | hell | light (e.g. **hellblau** means light blue) |
| schwarz | black | dunkel | dark (e.g. **dunkelbraun** means dark brown) |
| grau | grey | | |

## The Alphabet

| A | as in **Arm** | J | as in **'yott'** | S | as in **Essen** |
|---|---|---|---|---|---|
| B | as in **Baby** | K | as in **Karl** | T | as in **Tee** |
| C | as in **Zähne** | L | as in **Ellenbogen** | U | as in **U-Bahn** |
| D | as in **dänisch** | M | as in **Emden** | V | as in **faul** |
| E | as in **zehn** | N | as in **Ende** | W | as in **weh** |
| F | as in **Effekt** | O | as in **Ofen** | X | as in **X-Strahlen** |
| G | as in **geben** | P | as in **Peter** | Y | say **'üpsilon'** |
| H | as in **Haar** | Q | as in **Kuh** | Z | as in **Zettel** |
| I | as in **Igel** | R | as in **Erde** | | |

**Wie heißen Sie?**
What is your name?

**Wie schreibt man das?**
How do you spell it?

**Ich heiße Bissel. Das schreibt man B, I, zweimal S, E, L.**
My name is Bissel. You spell it B, I, double S, E, L.

# Essential German

## Being Polite

There are three words for 'you' in German: **du**, **ihr** and **Sie**.

You use **du** when speaking to a friend, a member of your family or an animal. For example:

- **Wo wohnst du?**
  Where do you live?

If you're speaking to more than one friend, family member or animal use **ihr**:

- **Kommt ihr?**
  Are you coming?

In a more formal situation, for example, speaking to a waiter, shopkeeper or stranger, you use **Sie**:

- **Guten Tag. Haben Sie Bananen, bitte?**
  Hello. Have you any bananas, please?

You use **Sie** for both singular and plural, i.e. whether you are addressing *one* person or *more than one* person.

## Greetings and Exclamations

| | | | |
|---|---|---|---|
| **Alles Gute** | All the best | **Herzlichen Glückwunsch** | Congratulations |
| **Auf Wiedersehen** | Goodbye | **Hi** | Hi |
| **Auf Wiederhören** | Goodbye (on phone) | **Ja** | Yes |
| **Bis bald** | See you soon | **Mit (großem) Vergnügen** | With (great) pleasure |
| **Bis später / morgen** | See you later / tomorrow | **Nein** | No |
| **Bitte** | Please / You're welcome | **Schöne Ferien** | Enjoy your holidays |
| **Danke (schön)** | Thank you (very much) | **Stimmt** | Right |
| **Entschuldigung** | Excuse me | **Tschüs** | Bye |
| **Es tut mir Leid** | I'm sorry | **Verzeihung** | Pardon me |
| **Gern geschehen** | Don't mention it | **Viel Glück** | Good luck |
| **Grüß Gott** | Hello | **Wie geht es dir / Ihnen?** | How are you? |
| **Hallo** | Hello | **Wie bitte?** | What did you say? |
| **Herzlich willkommen** | Welcome | | |

## Useful Phrases

| | | | |
|---|---|---|---|
| **Auf diese Weise** | In this way | **gerade** | just |
| **Das ist mir egal** | I don't care / mind | **gewöhnlich** | usually |
| **Das kommt darauf an** | It depends | **in Ordnung** | okay |
| **Das macht nichts** | It doesn't matter | **meiner Meinung nach** | in my opinion |
| **Das reicht** | I've had enough | **Mir geht's gut / schlecht** | I'm fine / unwell |
| **Ich habe es eilig** | I am in a hurry | **natürlich** | of course |
| **Es gibt** | there is / there are | **noch einmal** | once again |
| **Es hängt davon ab** | It depends | **Schade** | (what a) shame |

## Question Words

| | | | |
|---|---|---|---|
| **Wann?** | When? | **Wie?** | How? |
| **Was?** | What? | **Wieviel?** | How much? |
| **Wer? / Wen? / Wem?** | Who? / Whom? / To whom? | **Wieviele?** | How many? |
| **Welcher? / Welche? / Welches?** | Which? | **Wie lange?** | How long? |
| **Wo?** | Where? | **Was für?** | What sort of? |
| **Warum?** | Why? | | |

## Conjunctions and Connectives

| | | | | | |
|---|---|---|---|---|---|
| **aber** | however / but | **das heißt** | that's to say | **und** | and |
| **also** | so / therefore | **dazu** | moreover | **während** | while / whereas |
| **auch** | also / too | **doch** | yet | **wahrscheinlich** | probably |
| **auch wenn** | even if | **erstens** | firstly | **wegen** | because of / owing to |
| **auf der einen Seite** | on the one hand | **natürlich** | obviously | **weil** | because |
| **auf der anderen Seite** | on the other hand | **oder** | or | **wenn** | when |
| **außer** | apart from / except | **seit** | since | **wie** | as / like |
| **danach** | afterwards | **seitdem** | since | **zum Beispiel** | for example |
| **dank** | thanks to | **so** | so | | |
| **dann** | then | **sobald** | as soon as | | |

## Common Abbreviations

| | |
|---|---|
| **Abi (Abitur)** | school leaving exam |
| **ADAC** | German motorists' organisation |
| **ARD** | German television company |
| **BRD** | (Bundesrepublik) Federal Republic of Germany |
| **CD-ROM** | CD-ROM |
| **DB** | German railway company |
| **d.h.** | i.e. |
| **EU** | European Union |
| **gem.** | according to |
| **GmbH** | Ltd |
| **ICE** | Inter-City-Express |
| **inkl.** | included |
| **KFZ** | motor vehicle |
| **LKW** | lorry |
| **MWSt** | value added tax |
| **NRW** | Nord-Rhein-Westfalen |
| **PLZ** | post code |
| **usw.** | etc. |
| **z.B.** | e.g. |
| **ZDF** | German television company |

## Quick Test

1. Say / write it in English:
   a) **Heute ist der vierundzwanzigste Juni.**
   b) **Es ist jetzt siebzehn Uhr fünfzehn.**
2. Say / write it in German:
   a) My name is Jonathan. It's spelt J-O-N-A-T-H-A-N.
   b) Excuse me. Where is the station?

# Personal Information and Family

## Members of the Family and Pets

Here are some useful words for describing members of your family and your pets:

| | | | |
|---|---|---|---|
| **das Baby** | baby | **der Goldfisch** | goldfish |
| **der Bruder** | brother | **der Hund** | dog |
| **der Cousin** | cousin (male) | **das Kaninchen** | rabbit |
| **das Enkelkind** | grandchild | **die Katze** | cat |
| **die Frau** | wife / woman | **die Maus** | mouse |
| **die Geschwister** | brothers and sisters | **das Meerschweinchen** | guinea pig |
| **die Großeltern** | grandparents | **das Pferd** | horse |
| **die Großmutter** | grandmother | **die Schildkröte** | tortoise |
| **der Junge** | boy | **der Vogel** | bird |
| **das Mädchen** | girl | | |
| **der Mann** | man / husband | | |
| **die Mutter** | mother | | |
| **die Schwester** | sister | | |
| **der Schwager** | brother-in-law | | |
| **die Schwägerin** | daughter-in-law | | |
| **der Sohn** | son | | |
| **die Tochter** | daughter | | |
| **der Vater** | father | | |
| **der Vati** | dad | | |

## Gender, Singular and Plural

German nouns are either masculine, feminine or neuter. You can tell what gender a noun is by the article in front of it.

**Der** **Vater** and **der** **Bruder** are both masculine, as you would expect, but so are **der** **Vogel** and **der** **Fisch**.

**Die** **Frau** and **die** **Mutter** are, of course, feminine, but so are **die** **Maus** and **die** **Katze**.

**Das Pferd** is neuter, but so is **das** **Mädchen**.

You use **die** for the plural for all genders. Remember, there are several different ways of forming the plural in German.

Most feminine nouns add **-en**:
**eine Frau** one woman ➡ **zwei Frauen** two women

Many masculine nouns add an Umlaut and / or **-e**:
- **ein Bruder** ➡ **zwei Brüder**
  (a brother) (two brothers)
- **ein Hund** ➡ **zwei Hunde**
  (a dog) (two dogs)
- **mein Plan** ➡ **meine Pläne**
  (my plan) (my plans)

Many neuter nouns add **-er** and / or an Umlaut:
- **ein Kind** (one child) ➡ **zwei Kinder** (two children)

*N.B. In this revision guide, the most common plurals are given in the word lists. In dictionaries the plural form is often given in brackets after the noun. Learn as many plural forms as you can as you go along.*

# Personal Information and Family

## Talking about Yourself

Here are some expressions you could use to introduce either yourself or others:

**Ich heiße**…    I am called / My name is…
**Ich bin**…    I am…
**Ich habe**…    I have…

**Er / Sie heißt**…    He / She is called…
**Er / Sie ist**…    He / She is…
**Er / Sie hat**…    He / She has…

**Mein Vorname ist… und mein Familienname ist…**
My first name is… and my surname is…

**Ich habe einen Bruder und eine Schwester.**
I have one brother and one sister.

**Ich habe zwei Schwestern aber ich habe keine Brüder.**
I have two sisters, but I have no brothers.

**Ich bin ein Einzelkind.**
I am an only child.

**Meine Brüder / Meine Schwestern heißen… und…**
My brothers / sisters are called… and…

**Ich bin fünfzehn Jahre alt.**
I am fifteen years old.

**Mein Vater / Meine Mutter ist vierzig Jahre alt.**
My father / My mother is forty years old.

## How to Say 'My', 'Your', 'His' and 'Her'

To say 'my', 'your', 'his' and 'her' in German you need to know if the word you're describing is masculine, feminine, neuter or plural.

Masculine – use **mein**  ➡  **mein Bruder**
Feminine – use **meine**  ➡  **meine Schwester**
Neuter – use **mein**  ➡  **mein Kind**
Plural – use **meine**  ➡  **meine Eltern**

(See p.23 for more information.)

These words follow the same pattern:

| | |
|---|---|
| **dein** | your |
| **sein** | his |
| **ihr** | her, their |
| **unser** | our |
| **euer** | your |
| **Ihr** | your |

## Quick Test

**1** Say / write it in English:
   **a) Mein Vater ist neununddreißig Jahre alt.**
   **b) Meine Mutter heißt Laura.**
   **c) Meine Schwester hat ein Kaninchen.**
   **d) Ich habe zwei Brüder aber keine Schwestern.**

**2** Say / write it in German:
   **a)** My father is forty-five.
   **b)** My mother has a brother.
   **c)** I am an only child.
   **d)** My sister has a horse.

# Describing Family and Friends

## 'Haben' und 'Sein'

Haben and sein are very important verbs. They're very useful when you want to describe yourself or someone else. Make sure you know these two verbs in full:

| haben | (to have) | sein | (to be) |
|---|---|---|---|
| ich habe | I have | ich bin | I am |
| du hast | You have | du bist | You are |
| er / sie / es hat | He / She / It has | er / sie / es ist | He / She / It is |
| wir haben | We have | wir sind | We are |
| ihr habt | You have | ihr seid | You are |
| sie haben | They have | sie sind | They are |
| Sie haben | You have | Sie sind | You are |
| | | | |
| ich hatte | I had | ich war | I was |
| du hattest | You had | du warst | You were |
| er / sie / es hatte | He / She / It had | er / sie / es war | He / She / It was |
| wir hatten | We had | wir waren | We were |
| ihr hattet | You had | ihr wart | You were |
| sie hatten | They had | sie waren | They were |
| Sie hatten | You had | Sie waren | You were |

**Ich bin fünfzehn, aber meine Freundin ist vierzehn.**
I am fifteen, but my friend is fourteen.

**Ich habe zwei Schwestern, aber mein Freund hat drei Brüder.**
I have two sisters, but my friend has three brothers.

**Seine Brüder sind dumm.**
His brothers are stupid.

## Describing People

Here are some useful adjectives to use when describing people:

| | | | |
|---|---|---|---|
| ärgerlich | annoying | gesund | healthy |
| artig | well behaved | glücklich | happy |
| attraktiv | attractive | goldig | charming |
| aufregend | exciting | groß | big / tall |
| ausgezeichnet | excellent | gut | good |
| böse | angry | gut gelaunt | in a good mood |
| dick | fat | häßlich | ugly / horrible |
| dreckig | dirty | hübsch | pretty |
| dumm | stupid | intelligent | intelligent |
| dynamisch | dynamic | jung | young |
| ekelhaft | disgusting | klein | small |
| ernst | serious | klug | clever |
| erfolgreich | successful | komisch | funny |
| fantastisch | fantastic | krank | ill |
| faul | lazy | launisch | moody |
| fit | fit | lebhaft | lively |
| fleißig | hard-working | laut | noisy |
| frech | cheeky | lustig | funny |
| geduldig | patient | müde | tired |

| | |
|---|---|
| reich | rich |
| schlecht | bad |
| schlank | slim |
| schön | beautiful |
| schüchtern | shy |
| schwach | weak |
| sicher | confident |
| sparsam | thrifty |
| sportlich | sporty / athletic |
| stark | strong |
| verheiratet | married |
| zornig | angry |

# Describing Family and Friends

## Describing People (cont.)

| | | | |
|---|---|---|---|
| **Ich habe**… | I have… | **blaue Augen** | blue eyes |
| **Er / Sie hat**… | He / She has… | **braune Augen** | brown eyes |
| | | **graue Augen** | grey eyes |
| **lange Haare** | long hair | **große Augen** | big eyes |
| **kurze Haare** | short hair | | |
| **blonde Haare** | blond hair | **Er hat**… | He has… |
| **schwarze Haare** | black hair | **einen Bart** | a beard |
| **braune Haare** | brown hair | **einen Schnurrbart** | a moustache |
| **glatte Haare** | straight hair | **eine Glatze** | a bald head |
| **graue Haare** | grey hair | | |
| **rote Haare** | red hair | **Er / Sie trägt eine Brille.** | |
| **lockige Haare** | curly hair | He / She wears glasses. | |
| **keine Haare** | no hair | | |
| | | **Seine / Ihre Persönlichkeit ist**… | |
| | | His / Her personality is… | |

## Finding Out About Others

As well as telling other people about yourself and your family, you'll want to find out about the person you're talking to. You'll need to ask questions like these:

**Wie heißt du / Wie heißen Sie?**
What is your name?

**Wie alt bist du / sind Sie?**
How old are you?

**Wann hast du / haben Sie Geburtstag?**
When is your birthday?

**Wo wohnst du / wohnen Sie?**
Where do you live?

**Wie sind deine / Ihre Augen?**
What are your eyes like?

**Wie sind deine / Ihre Haare?**
What is your hair like?

**Hast du / Haben Sie Geschwister?**
Do you have any brothers or sisters?

## Quick Test

**1** Say / write it in English:
   a) **Mein Vater hat kurze Haare.**
   b) **Meine Mutter ist sehr schlank.**
   c) **Meine Schwester hat braune Augen.**

**2** Say / write it in German:
   a) My brother has long hair.
   b) I have black hair and brown eyes.
   c) How old is your sister?

# Character and Personality

## Relationships with Other People

Here are some verbs you can use to describe your relationships with other people:

| | |
|---|---|
| *aussehen | to appear |
| begegnen | to meet |
| beraten | to advise |
| besprechen | to discuss |
| besuchen | to visit |
| bevorzugen | to prefer |
| diskutieren | to discuss |
| gefallen | to please |
| auf die Nerven gehen | to get on (someone's) nerves |

| | |
|---|---|
| glauben | to think / believe |
| hassen | to hate |
| heiraten | to marry |
| kennen | to know |
| lächeln | to smile |
| lachen | to laugh |
| leben | to live |
| lieben | to love |
| lügen | to tell a lie |
| plaudern | to chat |
| raten | to advise |
| reden | to talk |
| telefonieren mit | to telephone |
| träumen | to dream |
| weinen | to cry |

*separable verb (see p.67)

## Using Verbs in the Present Tense

These are the different verb endings to use in the present tense:

| | |
|---|---|
| ich -e | ihr -t |
| du -st | sie -en |
| er / sie / es -t | Sie -en |
| wir -en | |

In addition, remember to change 'strong' verbs in the **du** and the **er / sie / es** forms. For example:

- **ich fahre**
  **du fährst**
  **er / sie / es fährt**

- **ich trage**
  **du trägst**
  **er / sie / es trägt**

- **ich nehme**
  **du nimmst**
  **er / sie / es nimmt**

You can find out if a verb is a strong verb by...
- looking at the list on pages 88–89
- looking at the lists in dictionaries.

If the verb appears in the list, it is strong. If it doesn't, then it isn't. Learn as many strong verbs as you can as you go along.

## Reflexive Verbs

When you use a reflexive verb, you need to add a reflexive pronoun to make the verb complete. The following are reflexive pronouns:

| | |
|---|---|
| mich | (myself) |
| dich | (yourself) |
| sich | (himself / herself / itself) |
| uns | (ourselves) |
| euch | (yourselves) |
| sich | (themselves) |
| sich | (yourself / yourselves) |

For example:
- **Ich amüsiere** mich    I have fun (i.e. amuse myself)
- **Er benimmt** sich    He behaves (himself)

Here are some reflexive verbs you can use when talking about relationships:

| | |
|---|---|
| sich amüsieren | to have fun |
| sich ärgern mit | to get angry with |
| sich benehmen | to behave |
| sich schämen | to be ashamed |
| sich streiten | to argue |
| sich verstehen | to get on with |

## Talking about Friends and Family

| | | | |
|---|---|---|---|
| allein | alone | ledig | single |
| einsam | lonely | tot | dead |
| geboren | born | treu | loyal |
| geschieden | divorced | unglücklich | unhappy |
| getrennt | separated | verliebt | in love |
| glücklich | happy | verwitwet | widowed |
| jung | young | zusammen | together |

**Mein Freund ist lustig und er lacht viel.**
My friend is funny and he laughs a lot.

**Meine Freundin ist immer glücklich, und wir reden immer.**
My friend is always happy and we talk all the time.

**Mein Bruder benimmt sich schlecht.**
My brother behaves badly.

## Personal Qualities and Flaws

| | | | |
|---|---|---|---|
| böse | angry | optimistisch | optimistic |
| deprimiert | depressed | pessimistisch | pessimistic |
| egoistisch | selfish | ruhig | peaceful / calm |
| eifersüchtig | jealous | stolz | proud |
| ein Sinn für Humor | a sense of humour | traurig | sad |
| freundlich | friendly | unhöflich | rude |
| gemein | nasty | verrückt | mad |
| lebendig | lively | zornig | angry |
| nett | nice | | |

## Quick Test

**1** Say / write it in English:
  a) **Mein Freund ist immer lustig.**
  b) **Mein Bruder ist egoistisch und gemein.**

**2** Say / write it in German:
  a) My father is friendly and always optimistic.
  b) My sister is sometimes jealous.

# Comparing People

## The Comparative

You can make comparisons by adding **-er** to any adjective:

**schnell** fast ➡ **schneller** faster
**klein** small ➡ **kleiner** smaller
**intelligent** intelligent ➡ **intelligenter** *more* intelligent

Use **als** for 'than'. For example:

- **Meine Schwester ist kleiner als ich.**
  My sister is smaller than me.
- **Ich bin intelligenter als mein Bruder.**
  I am more intelligent than my brother.

You usually need to add an Umlaut to the vowels **a**, **o** and **u** in the comparative adjective, so they become **ä**, **ö** and **ü**. For example:

- **Mein Freund ist jünger als ich.**
  My friend is younger than me.
- **Mein Vater ist älter als meine Mutter.**
  My father is older than my mother.

Learn these irregular comparatives as well:

**gut** good ➡ **besser** better
**hoch** high ➡ **höher** higher

## The Superlative

You can add **-ste** to any adjective to express the superlative:

- **der / die / das kleinste**... the smallest...
- **der / die / das lustigste**... the funniest...

As before, **a**, **o** and **u** in the superlative adjective usually become **ä**, **ö** and **ü**:

- **der / die / das größte**... the biggest...
- **der / die / das älteste**... the oldest...

Learn these irregular superlatives as well:

- **gut** good ➡ **der / die / das beste**... the best...
- **hoch** high ➡ **der / die / das höchste** the highest

> **Karl ist mein bester Freund.**
> Karl is my best friend.
>
> **Karl ist der lustigste Schüler in der Klasse.**
> Karl is the funniest boy in the class.
>
> **Suzi ist das älteste Mädchen.**
> Suzi is the oldest girl.

## More People to Talk About

| | | | | |
|---|---|---|---|---|
| **der Halbbruder** | half-brother | | **die Stiefschwester** | step-sister |
| **die Halbschwester** | half-sister | | **der Stiefvater** | step-father |
| **die Kusine** | (female) cousin | | **die Tante** | aunt |
| **die Nichte** | niece | | **der Vetter** | (male) cousin |
| **der Neffe** | nephew | | **der Zwilling** | twin |
| **die Oma** | granny | | | |
| **der Onkel** | uncle | | | |
| **der Opa** | granddad | | | |

**Schwieger** can't be used on its own, it must always be attached to another noun, for example:

- **Schwiegervater** father-in-law

## More about Reflexive Verbs

You have already revised reflexive verbs (see p.15).

Some reflexive verbs take a dative reflexive pronoun, usually when there is the meaning of doing something, 'to' or 'for' oneself. For example:

- **Ich bürste mir die Haare.**
  I brush my hair. ('I brush (for myself) the hair')
- **Willst du dir die Hände waschen?**
  Do you want to wash your hands?
  ('Do you want to wash (for yourself) the hands?')

The dative reflexive pronouns are as follows:
**ich** mir
**du** dir
**er / sie / es** sich
**wir** uns
**ihr** euch
**sie** sich
**Sie** sich

## Useful Tips for Your Examination

Here are some words that are very often muddled up by candidates in exams. Study them carefully and make sure you don't get caught out!

**wir** we ⟷ **wie** as / like
**man** one / we / people ⟷ **der Mann** man
**schön** beautiful ⟷ **schon** already
**wo?** where? ⟷ **wer?** who?
**also** therefore ⟷ **auch** also
**dann** then ⟷ **denn** because / for
**bekommen** to obtain ⟷ **werden** to become
**still** silent ⟷ **immer noch** still
**die Uhr** the clock ⟷ **die Stunde** the hour
**können** to be able to ⟷ **dürfen** to be allowed to

**ein paar** a few ⟷ **ein Paar** a pair / couple
**die Freude** joy ⟷ **die Freunde** friends
**die Kirsche** cherry ⟷ **die Kirche** church
**der Käse** cheese ⟷ **die Kasse** checkout
**ich mochte** I used to like ⟷ **ich möchte** I would like
**nicht** not ⟷ **nichts** nothing
**die Schwester** sister ⟷ **die Geschwister** brothers and sisters
**der Nachttisch** bedside table ⟶ **der Nachtisch** pudding / dessert

And remember, **ein Warenhaus** is a department store, not a warehouse!

## Tips for Speaking

The sounds that cause the most trouble to candidates in their speaking exam are **ch, z** and **st**. Check with your teacher if you are unsure of how to pronounce these sounds.

Practise saying out loud words that contain these sounds, so that you get used to pronouncing them in an authentic German way. Ask your teacher if you are unsure of any pronunciation.

For example:
- **ich, dich, mich, nach, noch, nicht, acht, Richtung, Fruchtsaft**
- **Zeit, Zeitung, zehn, zwanzig, zweiundzwanzig, Zwiebel**
- **Stunde, stehen, gestanden, verstehe, stimmt, Stress**

## Quick Test

**1** Say / write it in English:
   **a)** Meine Schwester ist kleiner als ich.
   **b)** Meine beste Freundin ist intelligenter als ich.
   **c)** Ihr Opa ist verwitwet.

**2** Say / write it in German:
   **a)** My best friend is a bit mad.
   **b)** My brother is never polite.
   **c)** My uncle is always good fun.

# Future Plans

## Wanting and Hoping

| | |
|---|---|
| **ich möchte** | I would like |
| **du möchtest** | You would like |
| **er / sie / es möchte** | He / She / It would like |
| **wir möchten** | We would like |
| **ihr möchtet** | You would like |
| **sie möchten** | They would like |
| **Sie möchten** | You would like |

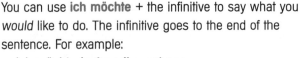

You can use **ich möchte** + the infinitive to say what you *would* like to do. The infinitive goes to the end of the sentence. For example:

- **Ich möchte in Amerika wohnen.**
  I would like to live in America.
- **Meine Schwester möchte als Krankenschwester arbeiten.**
  My sister would like to work as a nurse.

You can use **ich hoffe... zu** + the infinitive to say what you *hope* to do. **Hoffen** has regular endings (see p.14). The infinitive goes at the end of the sentence with **zu** in front of it. For example:

- **Ich hoffe, viele Kinder zu haben.**
  I hope to have lots of children.
- **Wir hoffen, viel Geld zu bekommen.**
  We hope to get lots of money.

## Talking about Future Plans

| | |
|---|---|
| **bekannt** | famous |
| **die Ehe** | marriage |
| **das Diplom** | diploma |
| **die Geburt** | birth |
| **glücklich** | happy |
| **gratulieren** | to congratulate |
| **die Hochzeit** | wedding |
| **die Hochschule** | college |
| **die Karriere** | career |
| **die Kinder** | children |
| **der Lebenslauf** | CV |
| **die Liebe** | love |
| **mein idealer Partner** | ideal partner (male) |
| **meine ideale Partnerin** | ideal partner (female) |
| **die Qualifikationen** | qualifications |
| **reich** | rich |
| **der Rentner** | pensioner |
| **der Trauring** | wedding ring |
| **verlobt** | engaged |
| **die Verlobung** | engagement |
| **die Universität** | university |
| **vielleicht** | perhaps |

## Useful Verbs

| | |
|---|---|
| **feiern** | to celebrate |
| **heiraten** | to marry |
| **sich freuen auf** | to look forward to |
| **sich verheiraten mit** | to get married to |
| **sich verloben mit** | to get engaged to |
| **studieren** | to study |
| **warten** | to wait |
| **werden** | to become |
| *__weitermachen__ | to continue |

*separable verb

## The Future Tense

Definite plans are what you *will do* in the future.

You use **werden** + the infinitive to say what you definitely will do. The infinitive goes to the end of the sentence. For example:

- **Ich werde auf die Universität gehen.**
  I will go to University.

Make sure you know how to use **werden**:

| | |
|---|---|
| **ich werde** | I will |
| **du wirst** | You will |
| **er / sie / es wird** | He / She / It will |
| **wir werden** | We will |
| **ihr werdet** | You will |
| **sie werden** | They will |
| **Sie werden** | You will |

## Useful Words

| | |
|---|---|
| **alte Leute** | old people |
| **das Baby** | baby |
| **der Beruf** | career / profession |
| **die Erwachsenen** | adults |
| **eine große Familie** | a large family |
| **junge Leute** | young people |
| **schwanger** | pregnant |
| **die Teenager** | teenagers |
| **die Verhältnisse** | relationships |

## Quick Test

**1** Say / write it in English:
   a) Ich möchte die ideale Partnerin finden.
   b) Ich hoffe, drei Kinder zu haben.
   c) Ich werde in Amerika arbeiten.

**2** Say / write it in German:
   a) I hope to become rich.
   b) I would like to study in America.
   c) I would like to be happy.

# Helping in Society

## Issues Affecting Society

Here are some useful words for describing issues that affect society:

| | | | |
|---|---|---|---|
| **die Agression** | aggression | **die Hautfarbe** | skin colour |
| **AIDS** | AIDS | **heutzutage** | nowadays |
| **der Alkohol** | alcohol | **HIV positiv** | HIV positive |
| **der Alkoholiker** | an alcoholic | **die Hungersnot** | famine |
| **der Alkoholismus** | alcoholism | **der Krieg** | war |
| **die Antwort** | answer | **der Lärm** | noise |
| **arbeitslos** | unemployed | **das Lotto** | lottery |
| **die Arbeitslosigkeit** | unemployment | **das Mobbing** | workplace bullying |
| **arm** | poor | **der Moslem / der Musulmann** | Muslim |
| **die Bedingungen** | conditions | **obdachlos** | homeless |
| **der Christ** | Christian | **der Obdachlose** | a homeless person |
| **der Dieb** | thief | **die Armut** | poverty |
| **der Diebstahl** | theft | **die Rasse** | race |
| **die Diskriminierung** | discrimination | **der Rassismus** | racism |
| **der Einwanderer** | immigrant | **die Rechte** | rights |
| **der Einwohner** | inhabitant | **der Rowdy** | thug |
| **die Freiheit** | freedom | **der Streik** | strike |
| **die Gastfreundschaft** | hospitality | **ungerecht** | unjust |
| **die Gefahr** | danger | **die Umfrage** | survey |
| **die Gesellschaft** | society | **der Vandalismus** | vandalism |
| **die Gleichheit** | equality | **die Wahrheit** | truth |
| **global** | global | | |

## Using 'Man'

In German you can use the pronoun **man** when you are not referring to a specific person. You can translate **man** as 'one, 'people', 'we' or 'you'.

| **Man muss…** | We / People must… |
|---|---|
| **Man kann…** | One / You can… |

## Other Useful Constructions

**Man soll…** + the *infinitive*   One should
**Man könnte…** + the *infinitive*   One could
**Man will…** + the *infinitive*   One wants to
**Man wollte…** + the *infinitive*   One wanted to

All of these verbs are followed by an infinitive. Remember to send the infinitive to the end of the sentence. For example:

- **Man muss Arbeit für die Arbeitslosen finden.**
  We must find work for the unemployed.
- **Man sollte mehr für die Obdachlosen tun.**
  We should do more for the homeless.
- **Man will Rechte haben.**
  People want to have rights.

## Tackling Issues Affecting Society

| | | | | |
|---|---|---|---|---|
| helfen | to help | | rassistisch | racist |
| bedauern | to regret | | schädlich | harmful |
| behalten | to keep | | sich beschweren | to complain |
| bekämpfen | to attack / combat / fight | | stören | to disturb |
| sich beklagen über | to complain about | | vermeiden | to avoid |
| benachteiligen | to disadvantage | | widmen | to devote / commit |
| drohen | to threaten | | verbergen | to hide |
| Es handelt sich um… | it's about… | | protestieren | to protest |
| kämpfen gegen | to fight against | | | |
| leisten | to achieve | | | |
| organisieren | to organise | | | |

**Man kann das Problem nicht vermeiden.**
We can't avoid the problem.

**Man soll die Kinder schützen.**
We should protect the children.

**Wenn man gegen die Armut kämpfen will, kann man freiwillig für die Obdachlosen arbeiten.**
If you want to fight poverty, you can work voluntarily for the homeless.

**Wir wollen keine rassistische Gesellschaft haben.**
We don't want to have a racist society.

**Es handelt sich nicht um die Hautfarbe, sondern um Rechte und Gleichheit.**
It's not about the colour of one's skin, but about rights and equality.

## Quick Test

1 Say / write it in English:
   a) Ich will mich über die Arbeitslosigkeit beschweren.
   b) Hier gibt es zu viel Obdachlosigkeit. Ich finde das unrecht.
   c) Man sollte gegen Rassismus kämpfen.

2 Say / write it in German:
   a) People want to fight famine.
   b) One problem is discrimination.
   c) We should protect their rights.

# House and Home

## Describing your House

| | | | |
|---|---|---|---|
| das Badezimmer | bathroom | der Rasen | lawn |
| der Balkon | balcony | das Reihenhaus | terraced house |
| der Baum | tree | der Schlafraum | bedroom |
| die Blume | flower | das Schlafzimmer | bedroom |
| das Büro | study | die Toilette | toilet |
| das Dach | roof | unten | downstairs |
| der Dachboden | attic / loft | die Waschküche | laundry room |
| die Essecke | dining area | das Wohnzimmer | lounge / living room |
| das Esszimmer | dining room | das Zimmer | room |
| der Fernsehraum | TV room | zu Hause | at home |
| die Garage | garage | | |
| der Garten | garden | der Haushalt | housework |
| das Gebäude | building | abwaschen | to wash up |
| das Gras | grass | aufräumen | to tidy up |
| das Haus | house | die Betten machen | to make the beds |
| das Heim | home | bügeln | to iron |
| das Hochhaus | high-rise building | *einkaufen | to go shopping |
| die Hütte | shed | im Garten arbeiten | to do the gardening |
| im Erdgeschoss | on the ground floor | kochen | to cook |
| im ersten Stock | on the first floor | mit dem Hund *spazierengehen | to walk the dog |
| der Keller | cellar | den Müll *hinaustragen | to put out the bin |
| die Küche | kitchen | putzen | to clean |
| der Mehrzweckraum | utility room | *staubsaugen | to do the vacuuming |
| möbliert | furnished | den Tisch *abdecken | to clear the table |
| oben | upstairs | den Tisch decken | to set the table |
| | | die Wäsche waschen | to do the washing |

*separable verb (see p.67)*

## How Often?

| | | |
|---|---|---|
| selten | rarely | **Ich decke jeden Tag den Tisch.** |
| ab und zu | from time to time | I set the table every day. |
| einmal pro Woche | once a week | |
| gewöhnlich | usually | **Ich koche nie.** |
| jeden Tag | every day | I never cook. |
| manchmal | sometimes | |
| nie | never | **Normalerweise mache ich die Betten.** |
| normalerweise | normally | Normally I make the beds. |
| oft | often | |
| regelmässig | regularly | |
| zweimal pro Woche | twice a week | |

## The Cases

|  | Masculine | Feminine | Neuter | Plural |
|---|---|---|---|---|
| Nominative | der | die | das | die |
| Accusative | den | die | das | die |
| Genitive | des | der | des | der |
| Dative | dem | der | dem | den |

|  | Masculine | Feminine | Neuter | Plural |
|---|---|---|---|---|
| Nominative | ein | eine | ein | meine |
| Accusative | einen | eine | ein | meine |
| Genitive | eines | einer | eines | meiner |
| Dative | einem | einer | einem | meinen |

These words take the same endings as **ein**:

| **mein** | my |
|---|---|
| **dein** | your |
| **sein** | his |
| **ihr** | her |
| **unser** | our |
| **euer** | your |
| **ihr** | your |
| **Ihr** | your |
| **kein** | not a / no… |

| **Mein Bruder** | my brother |
|---|---|
| **Unsere Familie** | our family |

Use the *nominative case* for the subject of the sentence:
- **Mein Vater deckt den Tisch**.
  My father sets the table.

Use the *accusative case* for the object of the sentence and after certain prepositions (see p.54):
- **Mein Vater deckt den Tisch**.
  My father sets the table.
- **Die Garage ist für das Auto**.
  The garage is for the car.

Use the *genitive case* to mean 'of the':
- **Das Schlafzimmer meines Bruders**.
  My brother's bedroom. (The bedroom of my brother)

Use the *dative* case after certain prepositions (see p.54):
- **Wir essen in der Küche**.
  We eat in the kitchen.

Remember, you need to add **-s** or **-es** masculine and neuter nouns in the genitive singular.

You need to add **-n** or **-en** to all nouns in the dative plural if they do not already end in **-n**.

## Quick Test

1. Say / write it in English:
   a) **Mein Schlafzimmer ist im ersten Stock.**
   b) **Ich decke regelmässig den Tisch und ich koche oft.**
   c) **Die Toilette ist unten.**

2. Say / write it in German:
   a) The garden is quite big.
   b) My house number is 14.
   c) I cook often, but I never iron.

# House and Home

## What is in Your House?

| | | | | |
|---|---|---|---|---|
| das **Abspülbecken** | sink | | das **Regal** | shelf |
| das **Bad / die Badewanne** | bath (tub) | | der **Schrank** | cupboard |
| das **Badetuch** | towel | | die **Schublade** | drawer |
| das **Bett** | bed | | der **Sessel** | armchair |
| der **Boden** | floor | | das **Sofa** | sofa |
| das **Bücherregal** | bookcase | | der **Spiegel** | mirror |
| die **Bürste** | brush | | der **Stuhl** | chair |
| der **Computer** | computer | | das **Telefon** | telephone |
| die **Decke** | ceiling | | die **Terrasse** | patio |
| die **Dusche** | shower | | der **Tiefkühlschrank** | freezer |
| der **Elektroherd** | electric cooker | | die **Tiefkühltruhe** | freezer |
| die **Etagenbetten** | bunk beds | | der **Tellerwäscher** | a person who washes dishes |
| das **Fenster** | window | | | |
| das **Fernsehgerät** | TV | | der **Teppich** | carpet / rug |
| der **Gasherd** | gas cooker | | die **Tischdecke** | table cloth |
| die **Geschirrspülmaschine** | dishwasher | | das **Tischtuch** | table cloth |
| die **Kommode** | chest of drawers | | die **Treppe** | stairs |
| das **Kopfkissen** | pillow | | die **Tür** | door |
| der **Kühlschrank** | fridge | | die **Uhr** | clock |
| die **Lampe** | lamp | | der **Vorhang** | curtain |
| die **Mauer** | wall | | die **Wand** | wall |
| der **Mikrowellenherd** | microwave | | das **Waschbecken** | basin |
| das **Möbelstück** | piece of furniture | | der **Wecker** | alarm clock |
| die **Möbel** | furniture | | die **Zahnpasta** | toothpaste |
| der **Nachttisch** | bedside table | | die **Zentralheizung** | central heating |

## Adjective Endings

You will gain high marks if you use adjective endings accurately in your exam.

Table 1 shows the adjective endings you would use after **ein**, **eine**, **dein**, **sein**, **unser**, **ihr**, **euer**, **Ihr** and **kein** (see p.23).

Table 2 shows the adjective endings you would use after **der**, **welcher**, **dieser** and **jener** (see p.57).

> **Karl ist ein guter Freund.**
> Karl is a good friend.
>
> **Unser neues Haus ist in London.**
> Our new house is in London.
>
> **Die alte Spülmaschine funktioniert nicht mehr.**
> The old dishwasher doesn't work any longer.

| Table 1 | Masculine | Feminine | Neuter | Plural |
|---|---|---|---|---|
| Nominative | -er | -e | -es | -en |
| Accusative | -en | -e | -es | -en |
| Genitive | -en | -en | -en | -en |
| Dative | -en | -en | -en | -en |

| Table 2 | Masculine | Feminine | Neuter | Plural |
|---|---|---|---|---|
| Nominative | -e | -e | -e | -en |
| Accusative | -en | -e | -e | -en |
| Genitive | -en | -en | -en | -en |
| Dative | -en | -en | -en | -en |

## Describing Your Room

**Ich habe mein eigenes Zimmer. Es ist sehr bequem.**
I have my own room. It's very comfortable.

**In meinem Zimmer gibt es ein Bett, einen Stuhl und einen Computer.**
In my room there is a bed, a chair and a computer.

**Die Wände sind blau, und die Vorhänge sind gelb.**
The walls are blue and the curtains are yellow.

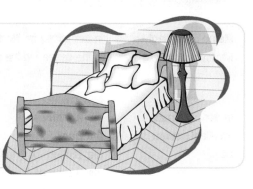

## Where Do You Live?

| | |
|---|---|
| **an der Küste** | at the seaside / on the coast |
| **auf dem Lande** | in the country |
| **auf einem Bauernhof** | on a farm |
| **in einem Doppelhaus** | in a semi-detached house |
| **am Stadtrand** | on the edge of town |
| **in der Stadtmitte** | in the town centre |
| **in den Bergen** | in the mountains |
| **im Vorort** | in the suburbs |
| **in der Nähe von einer Stadt** | near a town |
| **in einem Dorf** | in a village |
| **weit vom Meer** | a long way from the sea |
| **in einer Wohnung** | in a flat |
| **in einem Wohnblock** | in a block of flats |

## Daily Routine

| | | | |
|---|---|---|---|
| ***aufwachen** | to wake up | **sich *anziehen** | to get dressed |
| ***ausschlafen** | to have a lie in | **sich die Haare bürsten** | to brush one's hair |
| **das Haus verlassen** | to leave the house | **sich duschen** | to have a shower |
| **frühstücken** | to have breakfast | **sich waschen** | to have a wash |
| **ins Bett gehen** | to go to bed | **sich wecken** | to wake up |
| **nach Hause kommen** | to come home | | |

*separable verb (see p.67)

## Quick Test

1 Say / write it in English:
   **a) Unsere Wohnung ist in einem großen Wohnblock.**
   **b) Mein Haus liegt am Stadtrand nicht weit vom Meer.**
   **c) Wir essen immer im Esszimmer.**

2 Say / write it in German:
   **a)** I work in my bedroom.
   **b)** My sister comes home at five o'clock.
   **c)** We sit in the lounge and watch TV.

# Your Local Area

## Your Local Area

| **Meine Stadt liegt…**<br>My town is… | → | **in der Mitte / im Norden / im Süden / im Osten / im Westen**<br>in the centre / in the north / in the south / in the east / in the west | → | **von England / Deutschland**<br>of England / Germany |

**In der Stadtmitte /**
**Im Stadtzenrum**
**ist…**
In the town centre
there is / are… →

| | |
|---|---|
| die Apotheke | the chemist |
| die Bank | the bank |
| die Bibliothek | the library |
| die Bücherei /<br>   Buchhandlung | the book shop |
| die Brücke | the bridge |
| der Brunnen | the well / fountain |
| die Burg | the castle / fortress |
| das Denkmal | the monument |
| die Diskothek | the disco |
| die Drogerie | the chemist |
| die Einbahnstraße | the one-way street |
| das Einkaufszentrum | the shopping centre |
| der Fahrradweg | the cycle path |
| das Freibad | the open air pool |
| der Freizeitpark | the amusement park |
| das Gasthaus | the inn |
| die Fußgängerzone | the pedestrian precinct |
| das Hallenbad | the indoor pool |
| das Informationsbüro | the tourist information<br>   office |
| die Kirche | the church |
| die Kneipe | the pub |
| das Krankenhaus | the hospital |
| der Markt | the market |
| die Post | the post office |

| | |
|---|---|
| das Museum | the museum |
| der Palast | the palace |
| das Rathaus | the town hall |
| das Reisebüro | the travel agent |
| das Schloss | the castle |
| die Sparkasse | the bank |
| das Stadion | the stadium |
| der Stau | traffic jam |
| der Strand | the beach |
| das Theater | the theatre |
| viel Verkehr | a lot of traffic |
| der Zoo | the zoo |

| | |
|---|---|
| **Es ist …** | It is… |
| **eine Industriestadt** | an industrial town |
| **eine Handelsstadt** | a commercial town |
| **eine historische Stadt** | a historical town |
| **eine Touristenstadt** | a tourist town |
| | |
| **Es liegt… nördlich von…** | It's in the north of… |
| **südlich von…** | south of… |
| **westlich von…** | west of… |
| **östlich von…** | east of… |

## Modal Verbs

| **können** | | **mögen** | | **wollen** | |
|---|---|---|---|---|---|
| **ich kann** | I can | **ich mag** | I like | **ich will** | I want |
| **du kannst** | You can | **du magst** | You like | **du willst** | You want |
| **er / sie / es kann** | He / She / It can | **er / sie / es mag** | He / She / It likes | **er / sie / es will** | He / She / It wants |
| **wir können** | We can | **wir mögen** | We like | **wir wollen** | We want |
| **ihr könnt** | You can | **ihr mögt** | You like | **ihr wollt** | You want |
| **sie können** | They can | **sie mögen** | They like | **sie wollen** | They want |
| **Sie können** | You can | **Sie mögen** | You like | **Sie wollen** | You want |

When you use *modal verbs* you need another verb in the infinitive. Make sure you send the infinitive to the end of the sentence. For example:

* **Ich mag hier wohnen.**
  I like living here.
* **Man kann ins Kino gehen.**
  People can go to the cinema.
* **Man will ein neues Einkaufszentrum bauen.**
  They want to build a new shopping centre.

## Useful Verbs

| **arbeiten** | to work | **fahren** | to drive | **liegen** | to be situated / lie |
|---|---|---|---|---|---|
| **ausgehen** | to go out | **finden** | to find | **reisen** | to travel |
| **besuchen** | to visit | **gehen** | to walk | **suchen** | to look for |
| **einkaufen gehen** | to go shopping | **kaufen** | to buy | | |

## Saying What You Prefer

There are several useful expressions that can be used for saying what your prefer:

**gern**
with pleasure (i.e. liking to do something)
* **Ich gehe gern einkaufen.**
  I like going shopping.

**nicht gern**
with no pleasure (i.e. disliking to do something)
* **Ich gehe nicht gern in die Stadtmitte.**
  I don't like going to the town centre.

**lieber**
preferably (i.e. preferring to do something)
* **Ich gehe lieber ins Kino.**
  I prefer going to the cinema.

**liebsten**
* **Ich gehe am liebsten ins Theater.**
  I like going to the theatre best.

### Quick Test

1. Say / write it in English:
   a) **Unsere Stadt liegt im Norden.**
   b) **Es ist eine große Industriestadt.**
   c) **In der Stadtmitte ist eine Fußgängerzone.**
2. Say / write it in German:
   a) Our town is in the south.
   b) You can visit the zoo or the art gallery.
   c) I like the shopping centre and the indoor pool.

# Getting Around

## Useful Words

| | | | | | |
|---|---|---|---|---|---|
| **der Ausweis** | ID card | **der Fußgänger** | pedestrian | **die Straßenbahn** | tram |
| **das Auto** | car | **die Landkarte** | map | **die Tankstelle** | petrol station |
| **der Bus** | bus | **das Motorrad** | motorbike | **die U-bahnstation** | underground station |
| **die Bushaltestelle** | bus stop | **der Reisebus** | coach | | |
| **der Fahrer** | motorist | **der Reisescheck** | traveller's cheque | **das (öffentliche)** | (public) transport |
| **der Flug** | flight | **die Reisetasche** | bag | **Verkehrsmittel** | |
| **der Flughafen** | airport | **das Reiseziel** | destination | **die Wartezeit** | waiting time |
| **das Flugzeug** | plane | **die Richtung** | direction | **der Zug** | train |

## Asking for Directions

| | |
|---|---|
| **Entschuldigung** | Excuse me |
| **Wie komme ich zum / zur…?** | How do I get to…? |
| **Ist hier in der Nähe eine Bank?** | Is there a bank near here? |
| **Wo ist die nächste Tankstelle?** | Where is the nearest petrol station? |
| **Gehen Sie geradeaus / nach links / nach rechts** | Go straight on / left / right |
| **Nehmen Sie die erste Straße links / rechts** | Take the first left / right |
| **Nehmen Sie die zweite Straße links / rechts** | Take the second left / right |
| **Gehen Sie über die Brücke / Straße** | Cross the bridge / street |
| **Gehen Sie bis zur Ampel** | Go to the traffic lights |
| **Es ist auf der linken / rechten Seite** | It's on the left hand / right hand side |
| **An der Ecke / Kreuzung** | At the corner / crossroads |

## Travelling by Car

| | |
|---|---|
| **die Ausfahrt** | exit (e.g. from a motorway) |
| **die Autovermietung** | car hire |
| **das Benzin** | petrol |
| **die Bremsen** | brakes |
| **der Diesel** | diesel |
| **der Führerschein** | driving licence |
| **der Kreisverkehr** | roundabout |
| **das Lenkrad** | steering wheel |
| **der Motor** | engine |
| **das Parkhaus** | multi-storey car park |
| **die Panne** | breakdown |
| **das Rad** | wheel |
| **der Reifen** | tyre |
| **die Reifenpanne** | flat tyre |
| **reparieren** | to repair |
| **ein rotes Licht** | red light |

| | |
|---|---|
| **die Scheinwerfer** | headlights |
| **der Sicherheitsgurt** | seat belt |
| **die Tiefgarage** | underground car park |
| **die Umleitung** | diversion |
| **die Windschutzscheibe** | windscreen |
| **überqueren** | to cross |

**Die Bremsen funktionieren nicht.**
The brakes aren't working.

**Ich habe in der Schillerstraße eine Panne.**
I've broken down in Schiller Street.

## Giving Instructions

To give instructions to someone, you need to use the *imperative*.

If you're speaking to someone you would address as **du**, take the **du** form of the verb and knock off the '**-st**':
- **Geh**…!     Go…!
- **Nimm**…!     Take…!

If you're speaking to someone you would address as **ihr**, use the usual **ihr** form without the word '**ihr**':
- **Geht**…!     Go…!
- **Nehmt**…!     Take…!

If you're speaking to someone you would address as **Sie**, reverse the verb and the word **Sie**:
- **Gehen Sie**…!     Go…!
- **Nehmen Sie**…!   Take…!

## Travelling by Train

| | | | | | |
|---|---|---|---|---|---|
| **die Abfahrt** | departure | **die Fahrkarte** | ticket | **hin und zurück** | return |
| **die Ankunft** | arrival | **der Fahrkartenschalter** | ticket office | **die Information** | information |
| **der Ausgang** | exit | **der Fahrplan** | timetable | **der Koffer** | suitcase |
| **die Auskunft** | information | **der Fahrpreis** | fare | **kontrollieren** | to check tickets |
| **der Bahnhof** | train station | **der Fahrschein** | ticket | **der Notausgang** | emergency exit |
| **der Bahnsteig** | platform | **die Fahrt** | journey | **der Passagier** | passenger |
| **direkt** | direct | **der Gang** | corridor | **die Reise** | journey |
| **der Eingang** | entrance | **das Gepäck** | luggage | **die Rückfahrkarte** | return ticket |
| **die Einzelkarte** | single ticket | **die Gepäckaufbewahrung** | left luggage | **die Verbindung** | connection |
| **entwerten** | to stamp / validate (a ticket) | **das Gleis** | platform / track | **der Wartesaal** | waiting room |
| | | **der Hauptbahnhof (Hbf)** | main station | | |

## Buying a Ticket and Getting Information

**Eine Einzelkarte nach Köln bitte.**
A single ticket to Cologne, please.

**Wann fährt der nächste Zug nach München ab?**
What time does the next train for Munich leave?

**Von welchem Gleis?**
From which platform?

**Wann kommt der Zug an?**
What time does the train arrive?

**Ist es direkt, oder muss ich umsteigen?**
Is it direct or do I have to change?

### Quick Test

1. Say / write it in English:
   a) Gehen Sie geradeaus bis zur Ampel, dann nach links.
   b) Wo ist der Bahnhof bitte?
   c) Wann fährt der nächste Zug nach Ostende?
2. Say / write it in German:
   a) How do I get to the underground station?
   b) Is there a waiting room here?
   c) What time does the train arrive?

# Practice Questions

## Reading

**1** Choose one of the following adjectives to describe the people listed below:

**faul**   **ungeduldig**   **sportlich**   **launisch**   **fleißig**   **traurig**   **sparsam**

**a)** Meine Mutter ist fünfundvierzig aber sie spielt jeden Tag Tennis. ........................................

**b)** Meine Tante hat nicht viel Geld. Sie kauft immer billige Kleider. ........................................

**c)** Manchmal spricht meine Freundin mit mir, manchmal nicht. Das verstehe ich nicht! ........................................

**d)** Mein Schwager bleibt bis elf Uhr im Bett! ........................................

**e)** Seine Kusine kommt pünktlich in der Schule an und bekommt immer gute Noten. ........................................

**f)** Mein Opa hat es immer eilig. Er hat nie Zeit für mich. ........................................

**2** Read the passage below and answer the questions that follow, in English.

> **Karl spricht über seine Stadt.**
>
> **Meine Stadt liegt in Norddeutschland, nicht weit von Bremen. Es ist eine kleine Industriestadt. Im Stadtzentrum gibt es ein Einkaufszentrum, ein Sportzentrum, ein schönes Freibad, ein Theater, und ein Schloss. Man kann Wanderungen machen, einkaufen gehen oder Sport treiben. Ich wohne gern hier. Es gibt viel zu tun und zu sehen.**
>
> **Ich würde nicht gern auf dem Lande wohnen. Dort gibt es nichts zu machen, und es ist zu ruhig. In der Zukunft möchte ich in einer großen Wohnung im Ausland wohnen, vielleicht in England, weil ich sehr gern Englisch spreche.**

**a)** Where exactly is Karl's home town?

........................................................................................................................................

**b)** What does he say you can do there?

........................................................................................................................................

**c)** Does he like living there? Why is this?

........................................................................................................................................

**d)** What does he say about the countryside?

........................................................................................................................................

**e)** Where does he want to live in the future and why?

........................................................................................................................................

## Speaking

**3** Give a full response, in German, to each of the questions below. Say your answer out loud.

**a)** Wie alt bist du?  **b)** Wann hast du Geburtstag?  **c)** Wie ist dein Charakter?

**d)** Hast du Geschwister?  **e)** Kannst du dein Haus / deine Wohnung beschreiben?

**f)** Beschreibe die Gegend, wo du wohnst.  **g)** Wo würdest du lieber wohnen, in der Stadt oder auf dem Lande?

## Writing

**4** Imagine that you're the scriptwriter for a German film and you need to come up with an interesting character. Write about each of the following aspects of your character, in German.

**a)** The character's looks and personality.

**b)** The character's interests and his / her relationships with others.

**c)** Something unusual that the character likes doing.

**5** You're writing about your plans for the future. Write about each of the following, in German.

**a)** Say what you want to do after you finish school.

**b)** Say where you want to live in the future and why.

**c)** Describe which countries you would like to travel to.

# School and School Subjects

## School Subjects

| | | | |
|---|---|---|---|
| die Biologie | biology | die Technologie / Technik | technology |
| die Chemie | chemistry | das Theater | drama / theatre studies |
| das Deutsch | German | das Turnen | PE / gym |
| das Englisch | English | das Wahlfach | option |
| die Erdkunde | geography | das Werken | craft subjects |
| das Französisch | French | | |
| die Fremdsprachen | languages | | |
| die Geographie | geography | | |
| die Geschichte | history | | |
| die Informatik | IT | | |
| das Kochen | cooking | | |
| die Kunst | art | | |
| das Latein | Latin | | |
| die Mathe(matik) | maths | | |
| die Medienwissenschaften | media studies | | |
| die Musik | music | | |
| die Naturwissenschaften | science | | |
| das Pflichtfach | compulsory subject | | |
| die Physik | physics | | |
| die politische Weltkunde | citizenship | | |
| die Religion | RE | | |
| die Sozialkunde | sociology | | |
| das Spanisch | Spanish | | |
| der Sport | PE / sport | | |

## Giving Your Opinion

Here are some ways in which you can express positive and negative opinions:

| Positive | | Negative | |
|---|---|---|---|
| toll! | great! | Blödsinn! | rubbish! |
| interessant | interesting | entsetzlich | terrible |
| einfach | easy | langweilig | boring |
| großartig | splendid | schwer | hard / difficult |
| Es macht Spaß | It is fun / enjoyable | furchtbar | awful / terrible |
| mein Lieblingsfach | My favourite subject | mies | rubbish |
| nützlich | useful | nutzlos | useless |
| praktisch | practical | schwierig | difficult |
| Spitze! | great! | Der Lehrer / Die Lehrerin ist zu streng / schlechter Laune | The teacher is too strict / in a bad mood |
| Der Lehrer / Die Lehrerin ist nett / sympathisch / gut gelaunt | The teacher is nice / kind / in a good mood | Ich bin nicht gut in… | I am not very good at… |
| Ich bin gut in… | I am good at… | Mathe kann ich nicht leiden | I can't stand maths |

# School and School Subjects

## In School

| | | | | | |
|---|---|---|---|---|---|
| **die Aufgabe** | exercise | **das Lineal** | ruler | **die Schultasche** | school bag |
| **der Austausch** | an exchange | **die Noten** | marks / results | **das Semester /** | term |
| **der Bleistift** | pencil | **das Papier** | paper | **Trimester** | |
| **das Buch** | book | **die Pause** | break | **das Studium** | studies |
| **das Fach** | subject | **die Prüfung** | test / exam | **der Stundenplan** | timetable |
| **der Filzstift** | felt tip | **der Radiergummi** | rubber | **die Tafel** | board |
| **der Füller** | fountain pen | **die Resultate** | results | **der Taschenrechner** | pocket |
| **das Heft** | exercise book | **der Schreibblock** | note pad | | calculator |
| **die Kreide** | chalk | **das Schulbuch** | textbook | **der Unterricht** | lessons |
| **der Kuli** | ball-point pen | **der Schüler** | pupil (male) | **das Wörterbuch** | dictionary |
| **das Labor** | laboratory | **die Schülerin** | pupil (female) | **das Zeugnis** | school report |

## Talking About Your School

| | | | | | |
|---|---|---|---|---|---|
| **die Aula** | hall | **die Oberstufe** | sixth form | **die Stunde** | lesson |
| **der Flur** | corridor | **die Pause** | break | **die Turnhalle** | gym |
| **gemischt** | mixed | **die Realschule** | (type of) | **der Umkleideraum** | changing room |
| **die Gesamtschule** | comprehensive school | | secondary | **die Werkstatt** | workshop |
| **die Grundschule** | primary school | | school | | |
| **das Gymnasium** | grammar school | **die Schule** | school | | |
| **die Hauptschule** | secondary school | **der Schulhof** | playground | | |
| **der Hausmeister** | caretaker | **der Schulleiter** | head teacher | | |
| **die Kantine** | canteen | **der Schultag** | school day | | |
| **der Kindergarten** | nursery | **das Sekretariat** | secretary's | | |
| **das Labor** | lab | | office | | |

## Which Class Are You In?

**Ich bin in der...**
**I am in...** →

| | |
|---|---|
| **siebten Klasse** | Year 7 |
| **achten Klasse** | Year 8 |
| **neunten Klasse** | Year 9 |
| **zehnten Klasse** | Year 10 |
| **elften Klasse** | Year 11 |
| **zwölften Klasse** | Year 12 |
| **dreizehnten Klasse** | Year 13 |

N.B. 'Ordinal' numbers are sometimes written with a full stop, for example:

**in der 8. Klasse** ➡ **in der achten Klasse** ➡ in the eighth class (Year 8)

**der 17. Februar** ➡ **der siebzehnte Februar** ➡ the 17th February

### Quick Test

1. Say / write it in English:
   a) **Mein Lieblingsfach ist Englisch. Ich bekomme immer gute Noten.**
   b) **Erdkunde ist sehr langweilig. Der Lehrer ist zu alt.**
   c) **Die Stunden beginnen um halb neun.**

2. Say / write it in German:
   a) I like learning German. It is very interesting.
   b) I do not like maths. It is too difficult. It is rubbish!
   c) The food in the canteen is very good.

# School Uniform and School Rules

## Talking About School Uniform

| | | | |
|---|---|---|---|
| die Bluse | blouse | der Schlips | tie |
| das Hemd | shirt | die Schuhe | shoes |
| die Hose | trousers | die Schuluniform | school uniform |
| die Jacke | blazer | die Socken | socks |
| die Krawatte | tie | die Sportschuhe | trainers |
| der Lippenstift | lipstick | die Strumpfhose | tights |
| der Ohrring | earring | der Trainingsanzug | track suit |
| der Pullover | jumper | die Trainingsschuhe | trainers |
| der Rock | skirt | altmodisch | old fashioned |
| die Sandalen | sandals | bunt | brightly coloured |
| der Schal | scarf | schick | smart |

## More Modal Verbs

**sollen**

| | |
|---|---|
| ich soll | I should |
| du sollst | You should |
| er / sie / es soll | He / She / It should |
| wir sollen | We should |
| ihr sollt | You should |
| sie sollen | They should |
| Sie sollen | You should |

**dürfen**

| | |
|---|---|
| ich darf | I may |
| du darfst | You may |
| er / sie / es darf | He / She / It may |
| wir dürfen | We may |
| ihr dürft | You may |
| sie dürfen | They may |
| Sie dürfen | You may |

## School Rules

**Man muss...**
You must...

**Man darf...**
You are allowed to...

| | |
|---|---|
| fleißig arbeiten | work hard |
| anderen zuhören | listen to others |
| Hausaufgaben machen | do homework |
| höflich sein | be polite |
| pünktlich ankommen | arrive on time |
| in den Stunden aufmerksam sein | pay attention in lessons |
| die richtige Uniform tragen | wear the correct uniform |

**Man darf nicht...**
You are not allowed to... /
You must not...

| | |
|---|---|
| Kaugummi kauen | chew gum |
| in den Stunden sprechen | talk in lessons |
| Schmuck / Make-up tragen | wear jewellery / make-up |
| rauchen | smoke |
| Abfall fallen lassen | drop litter |
| unhöflich sein | be insolent / rude |
| die Schule schwänzen | play truant |

- **Wir dürfen Kaugummi nicht kauen.**
  We are not allowed to chew gum.
- **Wir müssen die richtige Uniform tragen.**
  We must wear the correct uniform.
- **Man darf die Schule nicht schwänzen.**
  You mustn't play truant.

# School Uniform and School Rules

## Useful Verbs

| | | | |
|---|---|---|---|
| **achten auf** | to pay attention to | **lernen** | to learn |
| **beantworten** | to answer | **lesen** | to read |
| **beenden** | to finish / end | **sagen** | to say |
| **beginnen** | to start | **schreiben** | to write |
| **beschreiben** | to describe | **schwatzen** | to chatter |
| **bestrafen** | to punish | **sich langweilen** | to be bored |
| **buchstabieren** | to spell | **sitzen bleiben** | to repeat a year |
| **durchfallen** | to fail | **sprechen** | to speak |
| **eine Frage stellen** | to ask a question | **tragen** | to wear |
| **fragen** | to ask | **unterrichten** | to teach |
| **gehören** | to obey | **verlassen** | to leave |
| **gelingen** | to succeed / pass | **verlieren** | to lose |
| **gewinnen** | to win | **zeichnen** | to draw |
| **Hausaufgaben machen** | to do homework | **zuhören** | to listen |
| **hassen** | to hate | **wiederholen** | to repeat / revise |
| **korrigieren** | to mark | | |

## German Word Order

You have to make sure that the main verb is always the *second idea* in any German sentence. For example:

- **In der Schule**    muss    **man**    **fleißig**    **arbeiten**.
  *1st idea*      *2nd idea…*

The infinitive is always the *final idea* and goes to the end of the sentence, for example:

- **Wir**    **dürfen**    **in der Schule**    **nicht**    rauchen.
                                          *final idea*

## Contractions

You can use any of these contractions in German, but be careful not to invent any others!

| | | |
|---|---|---|
| **aufs** | **auf das**… | onto the… |
| **ans** | **an das**… | to the… |
| **am** | **an dem**… | on the… |
| **beim** | **bei dem**… | at the house of the… |
| **durchs** | **durch das**… | through the… |
| **fürs** | **für das**… | for the… |
| **im** | **in dem**… | in the… |
| **ins** | **in das**… | into the… |
| **vom** | **von dem**… | from the… |
| **zum** | **zu dem**… | to the… |
| **zur** | **zu der**… | to the… |

### Quick Test

1. Say / write it in English:
   a) Die Jungen tragen eine schwarze Jacke und die Mädchen tragen einen blauen Rock.
   b) Wir müssen immer unsere Hausaufgaben machen.
   c) Wir sollen morgens immer pünktlich ankommen.
2. Say / write it in German:
   a) We are not allowed to wear earrings.
   b) The uniform is smart but a bit old fashioned.
   c) The boys in my class are always impolite.

## Pressure at School

| | | | |
|---|---|---|---|
| das Abschlusszeugnis | final report | die Durchschnittsnote | average mark |
| das Bullying | bullying | fehlen | to be absent |
| der Direktor | headteacher | der Fehler | mistake |
| die Disziplin | discipline | die Klassenarbeit | test |
| | | die mittlere Reife | GCSE (equivalent) |
| | | eine mündliche Prüfung | an oral exam |
| | | eine schriftliche Prüfung | a written exam |
| | | *nachsitzen | to do detention |
| | | die Noten | marks |
| | | die Prüfung | examination |
| | | rechnen | to count |
| | | der Schulabschluss | leaving certificate |
| | | der Schulbus | school bus |
| | | der Stress | stress |
| | | das Zeugnis | report |

*separable verb (see p.67)*

## More About the Infinitive

These are very useful expressions you can use with the infinitive: Remember – the infinitive goes *to the end.*

**ohne zu**... without...
**Ich mache diese Übungen, ohne daran zu denken.**
I do these exercises without thinking.

**um...zu** in order to
**Ich mache meine Hausaufgaben, um zu lernen.**
I do my homework in order to learn.

## More Useful Words

| | |
|---|---|
| die Ausbildung | education |
| die Berufsausbildung | vocational training |
| korrigieren | to mark |
| die Leistung | achievement |
| die Liste | list |
| das Maximum | maximum |
| das Minimum | minimum |
| der Morgen | morning |
| mühsam | painstaking |
| der Nachteil | disadvantage |
| okay | okay |

## Subordinating Conjunctions

Here are some useful conjunctions (also known as connectives):

| als | when | nachdem | after |
|-----|------|---------|-------|
| als ob | as if | ob | if |
| bevor | before | obwohl | although |
| bis | until | sodass... | with the result that... |
| da | as | während | while |
| damit | in order that | weil | because |
| dass | that | wenn | if |

When you use subordinating conjunctions, you must send the verb to the end of the sentence. For example:

- **Wir bekommen gute Noten, wenn wir fleißig arbeiten.**
  If we work hard we get good marks.
- **Du bekommst eine schlechte Durchschnittsnote, weil du keine Hausaufgaben machst.**
  You get a poor average mark because you do no homework.

## The Conditional Tense

When you want to say you *would* do something, you need to use the conditional tense.

To form the conditional tense...
- use the appropriate part of **würde** and an infinitive
- send the infinitive to the end of the sentence.

Here are the parts of **würde**:

| ich würde | I would |
|-----------|---------|
| du würdest | You would |
| er / sie / es würde | He / She / It would |
| wir würden | We would |
| ihr würdet | You would |
| sie würden | They would |
| Sie würden | You would |

**Ich würde gern nach Griechenland fahren.**
I would like to go to Greece.

**Würdest du Chinesisch sprechen?**
Would you speak Chinese?

For the verbs **sein** and **haben** you can use the imperfect subjective as an alternative to the normal conditional.

| ich wäre | I would be |
|----------|------------|
| du wärest | You would be |
| er / sie / es wäre | He / She / It would be |
| wir wären | We would be |
| ihr wäret | You would be |
| sie wären | They would be |
| Sie wären | You would be |
| | |
| ich hätte | I would have |
| du hättest | You would have |
| er / sie / es hätte | He / She / It would have |
| wir hätten | We would have |
| ihr hättet | You would have |
| sie hätten | They would have |
| Sie hätten | You would have |

## Quick Test

1. Say / write it in English:
   a) Peter muß nachsitzen, weil er schlechte Noten bekommen hat.
   b) Laura macht viele Fehler, weil sie nicht gut rechnen kann.
   c) Wir haben zuviel Stress in der Schule!

2. Say / write it in German:
   a) There is no bullying in my school and the discipline is quite good.
   b) The teachers work hard. They mark our work every week.
   c) My average mark was excellent!

# Plans After Leaving School

## Jobs

| | | | | |
|---|---|---|---|---|
| die / der Angestellte | employee | | der Klempner | plumber |
| der Apotheker | chemist | | der Krankenpfleger | nurse (male) |
| der Arbeitgeber | employer | | die Krankenschwester | nurse (female) |
| der Architekt | architect | | der Künstler | artist |
| der Arzt | doctor | | der Ladenbesitzer | shopkeeper |
| der Bäcker | baker | | der Lebensmittelhändler | grocer |
| der Bauarbeiter | builder | | der Lehrer | teacher |
| der Bauer | farmer | | der Manager | manager |
| der Beamte | official / civil servant | | der Maurer | bricklayer |
| der Briefträger | postman | | der Mechaniker | mechanic |
| der Elektriker | electrician | | der Pfarrer | vicar |
| der Fahrer | driver | | der Polizist | police officer |
| der / die Feuerwehrmann / frau | fireman / woman | | der Postbeamte | postman |
| der Fleischer | butcher | | der Priester | priest |
| der Friseur | hairdresser | | der Schauspieler | actor |
| der Gärtner | gardener | | der Sekretär | secretary |
| die Hausfrau / der Hausmann | housewife / husband | | der Steward | steward |
| der Informatiker | IT specialist | | der Techniker | technician |
| der Ingenieur | engineer | | der Tierarzt | vet |
| der Journalist | journalist | | der Verkäufer | shop assistant |
| der Kassierer | cashier | | der Vertreter | representative |
| der Kellner | waiter | | der Zahnarzt | dentist |

When you talk about a woman's job, you need to use the feminine version of the word. The usual way to do this is to add -in:

- **der Lehrer**    teacher (male)
  **die Lehrerin**    teacher (female)

You often add an Umlaut too:

- **der Arzt**    doctor (male)
  **die Ärztin**    doctor (female)

## Why do You Want to do that Job?

**Ich will Mechaniker(in) werden, weil ich mich für Autos interessiere.**
I want to become a mechanic because I am interested in cars.

**Ich will Tierarzt (-ärztin) werden, weil ich Tiere sehr gern habe.**
I want to become a vet because I love animals.

**Ich will Arzt (Ärztin) werden, um anderen zu helfen.**
I want to become a doctor in order to help others.

**Ich will auf einem Bauernhof arbeiten, weil ich gern im Freien bin.**
I want to work on a farm because I like to be in the open air.

JLS-523

## Useful Expressions

| | |
|---|---|
| ich interessiere mich für… | I am interested in… |
| eine Lehre | apprenticeship |
| der Lehrling | apprentice |
| berufstätig | working |
| dieses Jahr | this year |
| am Ende des Jahres | at the end of the year |
| bald | soon |
| in der Zukunft | in the future |
| in zwei Monaten | in two months |
| nach zwei Wochen / Jahren | in two weeks' / years' time |
| nächstes Jahr | next year |
| nächste Woche | next week |
| verbringen | to spend (time) |
| verlassen | to leave |

## More About Modal Verbs

These modal verbs in the imperfect tense are also useful:

- ich konnte… I could…
- ich wollte… I wanted to…
- ich mochte… I liked to…

Remember that the infinitive goes to the end of the sentence.

- **Als Kind wollte ich immer als Verkäufer arbeiten.**
  As a child I always wanted to work as a shop assistant.

## 'Weak' Nouns

'Weak' nouns are masculine nouns that add an **-n** to every case except the *nominative singular*. For example:

- *Nominative singular:* **Der Student arbeitet in diesem Büro.**
  The student works in this office.
- *Accusative singular:* **Dieser Brief ist für den Studenten.**
  This letter is for the student.
- *Nominative plural:* **Die Studenten arbeiten alle in diesem Büro.**
  The students are all working in this office.

Here are some other common 'weak' nouns:

| | |
|---|---|
| der Bauer | farmer |
| der Fotograf | photographer |
| der Franzose | Frenchman |
| der Junge | boy |
| der Polizist | policeman |

## Quick Test

1. Say / write it in English:
   a) Ich will Krankenschwester werden.
   b) Meine Freundin will auf die Universität gehen.
   c) Am Ende des Jahres hoffe ich, eine Lehre zu beginnen.
2. Say / write it in German:
   a) Next year I want to work as a mechanic.
   b) In two years' time I want to leave school.
   c) When I'm 21, I want to work abroad.

# Part-time Work and Pocket Money

## Part-time Work

| | | | |
|---|---|---|---|
| **arbeiten** | to work | **beginnen** | to begin |
| **babysitten** | to babysit | **bekommen** | to get / receive |
| **beantworten** | to answer | **dienen** | to serve |
| **beenden** | to finish | **helfen** | to help |
| | | **jobben** | to have a job |
| | | **kriegen** | to obtain |
| | | **liefern** | to deliver |
| | | **sorgen für** | to look after |
| | | **verdienen** | to earn |
| | | **von zu Hause arbeiten** | to work from home |
| | | *__vorbereiten__ | to prepare |
| | | **freiwillig** | voluntarily |
| | | **der Ganztagsjob** | full-time job |
| | | **der Nebenjob** | extra job / sideline |
| | | **die Teilzeitarbeit** | part-time job |
| | | **pro** | per |

*separable verb (see p.67)

## Adverbs – Comparative and Superlative

Remember, any adjective can also be used as an adverb:

- **Der Zug ist** schnell.
  The train is quick.
- **Der Zug fährt** schnell.
  The train goes quickly.

To form the comparative of any adverb you add -er:

- **Dieser Zug fährt** schneller.
  This train goes more quickly.

To form the superlative you use this form:
am (adverb)sten:

- **Der IC-Zug fährt** am schnellsten.
  The IC train goes the quickest.
- **Ich spreche gut Französisch und English aber ich spreche** am besten **Deutsch.**
  I speak French and English well but I speak German best.

## Pocket Money

**Mit meinem Taschengeld kaufe ich**…
With my pocket money I buy…

| | | | |
|---|---|---|---|
| **die CDs** | CDs | **das Make-up** | make-up |
| **das Essen** | things to eat | **der Schmuck** | jewellery |
| **die Geschenke** | presents | **das Schulmaterial** | things for school |
| **die Karten** | cards | **die Zeitschriften** | magazines |
| **die Kleider** | clothes | | |

**Ich will Geld sparen, um**…
I want to save money to…

| | |
|---|---|
| **auf Urlaub zu gehen** | go on holiday |
| **einen Computer zu kaufen** | buy a computer |
| **mir ein Fahrrad zu kaufen** | buy myself a bike |

**Ich muss zu Hause helfen, um Geld zu verdienen.**
I have to help at home to earn money.

**Meine Eltern geben mir Geld. Ich bekomme zehn Pfund pro Woche.**
My parents give me money. I get £10 per week.

### Quick Test

1. Say / write it in English:
   a) Ich mache Teilzeitarbeit in einem Café.
   b) Ich verdiene sechs Pfund pro Stunde.
   c) Mit meinem Taschengeld kaufe ich Schulmaterial und Zeitschriften.
   d) Wie kann ich am besten einen Nebenjob finden?
2. Say / write it in German:
   a) With my pocket money I buy presents and computer games.
   b) I want to save money in order to buy jewellery.
   c) I look after my young brother.
   d) My friend works from home.

# Jobs and Work Experience

## Talking about the Past – the Perfect Tense

To form the perfect tense, you need *two* parts: an *auxiliary* and a *past participle*.

**1** The auxiliary is either the verb **haben** or the verb **sein** (see p.12).

**2** To form the past participle first you need to know whether the verb is *strong* or *weak* (see p.14).

All weak verbs take **haben**.

Strong verbs that take **sein** are usually marked with an * in the strong verb list (p.88–89). Try to learn them as you go along.

## Past Participle – Strong Verbs

Look in the strong verb list (p.88–89) to find the past participle. Learn as many as you can as you go along.

|  | Auxiliary | Past Participle |  |
|---|---|---|---|
| **ich** | **bin**… | gefahren | I travelled |
| **ich** | **habe**… | *angerufen | I phoned |
| **ich** | **habe**… | begonnen | I started |
| **ich** | **habe**… | geholfen | I helped |
| **ich** | **habe**… | gelesen | I read |
| **ich** | **habe**… | geschrieben | I wrote |
| **ich** | **habe**… | getan | I did / made |

*separable verb (see p.67)

## Past Participle – Weak Verbs

When using weak verbs, take the infinitive…
* and knock off **-en**
* then add **ge-** to the beginning of the word and **-t** to the end of the word.

|  | Auxiliary | Past Participle |  |
|---|---|---|---|
| **ich** | **habe**… | gemacht | I made |
| **ich** | **habe**… | getippt | I typed |
| **ich** | **habe**… | gearbeitet | I worked |

Weak verbs that start with **be-**, **ver-** or **zer-** don't need **ge-**, for example:
* **ich habe** bedient — I served
* **ich habe** benützt — I used

Weak verbs that end in **-ieren** don't need **ge-** either, for example:
* **ich habe** kopiert — I copied
* **ich habe** repariert — I repaired

# Jobs and Work Experience

## Giving Your Opinion

**Im Allgemeinen war mein Arbeitspraktikum**…
Overall, my work experience was…

| | |
|---|---|
| **eine Zeitverschwendung** | a waste of time |
| **ermüdend** | tiring |
| **interessant** | interesting |
| **langweilig** | boring |
| **nützlich** | useful |
| **nutzlos** | useless |
| **praktisch** | practical |

**Der Firmenchef war**…
The boss was…

**Meine Kollegen waren**…
My colleagues were…

| | |
|---|---|
| **(un)freundlich** | (un)friendly |
| **(un)höflich** | (im)polite |
| **(un)sympathisch** | (un)kind |
| **angenehm** | pleasant |
| **beschäftigt** | busy |
| **blöd** | stupid |
| **fleißig** | hard working |
| **freundlich** | kind |
| **hilfsbereit** | helpful |
| **nett** | nice |

## Talking About Work

| | |
|---|---|
| **anders** | different |
| **am Anfang** | at the beginning |
| **gut / schlecht bezahlt** | well / badly paid |
| **wie geplant** | as planned |
| **die Akte** | folder / file |
| **der Anrufbeantworter** | answerphone |
| **der Arbeiter** | worker |
| **der Betrieb** | factory |
| **die Bezahlung** | pay |
| **bitten** | request |
| **der E111-Schein** | E111 |
| **das Gehalt** | salary |
| **die Konferenz** | conference |
| **der Kurs** | course |
| **das Marketing** | marketing |
| **die Stelle** | job |

- **Ich habe die Stellenangebote gesehen.**
  I have seen the job adverts.
- **Ich möchte mich um diese Stelle bewerben.**
  I would like to apply for this post.
- **Ich hatte eine Stelle in einem Altenheim.**
  I had a job in a retirement home.

### Quick Test

1. Say / write it in English:
   a) **Ich habe zwei Wochen in einem Büro gearbeitet.**
   b) **Ich habe kein Geld verdient, aber das Praktikum hat Spaß gemacht.**
   c) **Er hat seine Arbeitserfahrung gehasst. Es war eine Zeitverschwendung.**
2. Say / write it in German:
   a) I wrote letters and worked at the computer.
   b) I finished work at five thirty.
   c) I travelled each day by bus.

# Practice Questions

## Reading

**1** Read the passages by Dieter, Sabine, Erkan and Amira below and answer the questions that follow, in English.

> Für mich sind gute Noten sehr wichtig, weil ich eine gute Arbeitsstelle haben will. Es ist aber oft schwer, in der Schule zu arbeiten, weil einige Schüler doof sind. Das geht mir auf die Nerven. Die Lehrer aber sind sehr geduldig und hilfsbereit.
>
> Erkan

> Ich gehe gern in meine Schule. Ich habe viele Freunde, und wir haben viel Spaß. Aber die Bibliothek ist zu klein, und wir haben kein Schwimmbad.
>
> Dieter

> Ich hasse mein Gymnasium. Es ist zu stressig. Die Lehrer interessieren sich nur für die intelligentesten Schülerinnen und für sie sind nur Hausaufgaben und Prüfungen wichtig. Wir arbeiten fleißig und wir haben keine Zeit, uns zu amüsieren. Ich möchte am Wochenende Badminton spielen, aber ich habe keine Zeit dafür.
>
> Sabine

> In meiner Schule sind die Lehrer unhöflich. Sie haben keine Zeit für die Schüler und Schülerinnen und sie verstehen sich nicht gut mit uns. Deswegen bin ich traurig.
>
> Amira

**a)** Which two students don't speak well of their teachers? _____

**b)** Who would like better facilities at school? _____

**c)** Who complains about other pupils' bad behaviour? _____

**d)** Who thinks their school is too narrowly academic? _____

**e)** Who wants to get a good job? _____

**f)** Who thinks there is too much pressure? _____

**g)** Who has a good time with friends? _____

**h)** Why does Amira say she is sad? _____

## Speaking

**2** Give a full response, in German, to each of the questions below. Say your answer out loud.

**a)** Kannst du deine Schule beschreiben?

**b)** Beschreibe einen typischen Schultag!

**c)** Wie ist deine Uniform?

**d)** Was ist dein Lieblingsfach?

**e)** Warum?

**f)** Welches Fach machst du nicht gern?

**g)** Warum nicht?

**h)** Was willst du machen, wenn du die Schule verlässt?

**i)** Warum?

**j)** Welchen Beruf hast du gewählt?

## Writing

**3** Imagine you're the headteacher of a school, talking about your plans for the school. Write about each of the following, in German.

**a)** Describe the school as it is now.

........................................................................................................................

........................................................................................................................

........................................................................................................................

**b)** Say what changes you'd make to the subjects studied and the school day.

........................................................................................................................

........................................................................................................................

........................................................................................................................

**c)** Write about the benefits and disadvantages of the students wearing school uniform.

........................................................................................................................

........................................................................................................................

........................................................................................................................

**4** You're writing about your ideal job. Write about each of the following, in German.

**a)** Describe the type of job you'd like to do in the future.

........................................................................................................................

........................................................................................................................

........................................................................................................................

**b)** Say why you would like to do this job and what experience / qualifications you need in order to get it.

........................................................................................................................

........................................................................................................................

........................................................................................................................

**c)** Describe whereabouts you would like to work and why.

........................................................................................................................

........................................................................................................................

........................................................................................................................

# Health and Fitness

## When? How? Where?

When speaking or writing in German you must observe strict rules about word order.

To get it right, always think to yourself: *When?* then *How?* then *Where?*

For example:
- **Ich fahre** jeden Tag / mit dem Bus / in die Schule.
  I travel to school every day by bus.
- **Ich habe** gestern / mit meinen Freunden / im Park **Fußball gespielt**.
  Yesterday I played football in the park with my friends.

*N.B. The 'When? How? Where?' rule is very different from the normal word order in English. Don't be caught out!*

## Impersonal Verbs

Impersonal verbs are different from normal verbs because they only exist in the third person.
For example:
- **Es** tut weh.
  It hurts.
- **Mir ist** krank / unwohl / schwindlig / übel.
  I feel ill / unwell / dizzy / sick.

| **Was** tut weh? What hurts? → | **Mir tut das Bein** weh | My leg hurts |
|---|---|---|
| | der Bauch | stomach |
| | der Finger | finger |
| | das Gehirn | brain |
| | das Gesicht | face |
| | der Hals | neck |
| | die Hand | hand |
| | das Kinn | chin |
| | das Knie | knee |
| | der Kopf | head |
| | der Körper | body |
| | das Herz | heart |
| | der Magen | stomach |
| | der Mund | mouth |
| | die Nase | nose |
| | das Ohr | ear |
| | der Rücken | back |
| | die Schulter | shoulder |
| | der Zahn | tooth |

## Other Ways of Saying you Feel Unwell

| | |
|---|---|
| **Ich habe eine Erkältung** | I've got a cold |
| **Ich habe eine Grippe** | I've got flu |
| **Ich habe Fieber** | I've got a temperature |
| **Ich huste** | I cough |
| **Ich niese** | I sneeze |
| **Ich kann kaum atmen** | I can hardly breathe |
| **Ich kann nicht schlafen** | I can't sleep |
| **Ich esse nichts** | I'm not eating anything |
| **Ich habe keinen Appetit** | I've got no appetite |

## Describing 'When'

| | | | | | |
|---|---|---|---|---|---|
| **abends** | in the evenings | **manchmal** | sometimes | **selten** | rarely |
| **gewöhnlich** | normally / usually | **meistens** | most of the time | **sofort** | immediately |
| **immer** | always | **mindestens** | at least | **täglich** | dally |
| **jetzt** | now | **schon** | already | **wieder** | again |

## Your Health – Useful Expressions

| | | | | |
|---|---|---|---|---|
| **(sich) schneiden** | to cut (oneself) | | **die Medizin** | medicine |
| **die Ader** | vein | | **messen** | to measure |
| **baden** | to bathe | | **physisch** | physical |
| **der Durst** | thirst | | **das Problem** | problem |
| **\*einatmen** | to breathe in | | **putzen** | to clean (teeth) |
| **das Gefühl** | feeling | | **schlimmer** | worse |
| **die Gesundheit** | health | | **die Sprechstunde** | surgery |
| **Gute Besserung!** | Get well soon! | | **die Spritze** | injection |
| **das Hansaplast** | sticking plaster | | **der Termin** | appointment |
| **der Hunger** | hunger | | **der / das Virus** | virus |
| *separable verb (see p.67) | | | **die Vitamine** | vitamins |

*Gute Besserung!*

## Quick Test

1 Say / write it in English:
   a) **Mir tut der Magen weh.**
   b) **Mir ist immer schwindlig.**
   c) **Mir tut der Rücken weh.**
   d) **Ich möchte einen Termin machen.**
      **Wann ist die Sprechstunde?**

2 Say / write it in German:
   a) **My tooth hurts.**
   b) **My finger hurts. Today it is worse than yesterday.**
   c) **I feel sick most of the time.**

# Smoking and Drugs

## Smoking

| | | | | |
|---|---|---|---|---|
| **die Abstinenz** | abstinence | | **die Lust** | desire |
| **das Angebot** | offer | | **niemals** | never |
| *<u>**aufgeben**</u> | to give up | | **riechen** | to smell |
| **bleiben** | to stay | | **sich streiten** | to argue |
| **das Blut** | blood | | **sterben** | to die |
| **der Brauch** | need | | **der Streit** | argument |
| **brauchen** | to need | | **der Tabak** | tobacco |
| **das Etui** | case | | **ungesund** | unhealthy |
| **die Gelegenheit** | opportunity | | **unmöglich** | impossible |
| **genießen** | to enjoy | | **unzufrieden** | discontent |
| **der Krebs** | cancer | | **die Verantwortung** | responsibility |
| **leider** | unfortunately | | **verboten** | forbidden |
| | | | **wählen** | to choose |
| | | | **die Zigarette** | cigarette |

*separable verb (see p.67)

## Intensifiers

Using an intensifier gives more detail to what you are saying. You can put intensifiers in front of any adjective.

Here are some commonly used intensifiers:

| | | | |
|---|---|---|---|
| **ein bisschen** | a bit | **oft** | often |
| **ganz** | completely | **total** | totally |
| **sehr** | very | **unglaublich** | incredibly |
| **immer** | always | **viel** | a lot |
| **furchtbar** | terribly | **völlig** | completely |
| **mittel-** | half- | **wenig** | (only) a little |
| **nicht** | not | **ziemlich** | fairly |
| **nicht sehr** | not very | **zu (viel)** | too (much) |

**Sie ist sehr sportlich.**
She is very athletic.

**Er ist nicht sehr gesund.**
He is not very healthy.

**Sie ist furchtbar abhängig.**
She is terribly addicted.

## Drugs

| | | | |
|---|---|---|---|
| abhängig | addicted | der Gebrauch | use |
| der Alkohol | alcohol | genug | enough |
| alkoholisch | alcoholic | illegal | illegal |
| bedürftig | needy | der Klebstoff | glue |
| der Benutzer | user | die Krankheit | illness |
| betrunken | drunk | die Kriminalität | crime / criminality |
| chemisch | chemical | das Leben | life |
| der Dieb | thief | legal | legal |
| doof | daft, crazy | nervös | nervous |
| die Drogen | drugs | das Risiko | risk |
| Drogen nehmen | to take drugs | sniffen | to snort |
| der Drogenhändler | drug dealer | die Spritze | injection |
| der Drogensüchtige(r) | drug addict | spritzen | to inject |
| *einnehmen | to consume / take | stehlen | to steal |
| erleben | to experience | die Sucht | addiction |
| der Tabak | tobacco | die Tablette | tablet |
| | | unterstützen | to support |
| | | der Verbrauch | consumption |

*separable verb (see p.67)

**Drogen sind ein großes Problem in unserer Gesellschaft.**
Drugs are a big problem in our society.

**Drogen können zu Kriminalität führen.**
Drugs can lead to crime.

**Viele junge Leute nehmen Drogen, um wie ihre Freunde oder Freundinnen zu sein. Das finde ich doof!**
Lots of young people take drugs in order to be like their friends. I think that is crazy!

## 'Jemand' and 'Niemand'

**Jemand** (someone) and **Niemand** (no-one) take endings in the various cases:

| Nominative | jemand | niemand |
|---|---|---|
| Accusative | jemanden | niemanden |
| Dative | jemandem | niemandem |

- **Ich sehe niemanden.**
  I see no-one.

### Quick Test

1. Say / write it in English:
   a) **Ich rauche nicht. Das Risiko ist zu groß.**
   b) **Tabak ist total ungesund.**
   c) **Ein Drogensüchtiger verschwendet sein Geld.**
2. Say / write it in German:
   a) She smokes too much.
   b) Drugs lead to crime.
   c) Cigarettes smell awful.

# Food and Drink

## Food

| | | | |
|---|---|---|---|
| die Ananas | pineapple | das Bonbon | sweet |
| der Apfel | apple | der Braten | roast |
| die Aprikose | apricot | das Brot | bread |
| die Banane | banana | das Brötchen | roll |
| die Birne | pear | das Butterbrot | sandwich |
| der Blumenkohl | cauliflower | die Chips | crisps |
| der Champignon | mushroom | die Eier | eggs |
| die Erbsen | peas | das Eis | ice cream |
| die Erdbeere | strawberry | die Haferflocken | oats |
| das Gemüse | vegetables | der Käse | cheese |
| die Grapefruit | grapefruit | der Kaugummi | chewing gum |
| grüne Bohnen | green beans | die Kekse | biscuits |
| die Gurke | cucumber | der Kuchen | cake |
| die Himbeere | raspberry | die Margarine | margarine |
| die Karotte | carrot | die Nudeln | noodles |
| die Kartoffeln | potatoes | das Omelette | omelette |
| das Kompott | stewed fruit | die Pommes (frites) | chips |
| die Kirsche | cherry | der Reis | rice |
| der Kohl | cabbage | das Schaschlik | kebab |
| die Melone | melon | die (Schlag)sahne | (whipped) cream |
| das Obst | fruit | der Senf | mustard |
| die Orange | orange | das Spiegelei | boiled egg |
| der Pfeffer | pepper | die Suppe | soup |
| der Pfirsich | peach | die Torte | tart / flan |
| die Pflaume | plum | die Vanille | vanilla |
| der Pilz | mushroom | | |

| | |
|---|---|
| der Aufschnitt | cooked meats |
| die Bratwurst | sausage |
| die Currywurst | curry sausage |
| der Fisch | fish |

| | |
|---|---|
| der Rosenkohl | Brussels sprouts |
| das Sauerkraut | pickled cabbage |
| der Salat | salad / lettuce |
| der Spinat | spinach |
| die Tomate | tomato |
| die Weintraube | grape |
| die Zitrone | lemon |
| die Zwiebel | onion |

| | |
|---|---|
| das Fleisch | meat |
| die Forelle | trout |
| die Frikadelle | meat ball |
| das Hähnchen | chicken |
| der Hamburger | hamburger |
| das Kalbfleisch | veal |
| das Kotelett | cutlet |
| der Lachs | salmon |
| das Lamm | lamb |
| die Leberwurst | liver sausage |
| die Meeresfrüchte | seafood |
| der Schinken | ham |
| das Schnitzel | Schnitzel |
| das Schweinefleisch | pork |
| das Steak | steak |
| der Thunfisch | tuna |
| die Wurst | sausage / salami |

# Food and Drink

## Drinks

| | | | |
|---|---|---|---|
| das Bier (vom Fass) | (draught) beer | das Pils | lager |
| die Cola | Cola | der Saft | juice |
| der Kaffee | coffee | die Schokolade | chocolate |
| der Kakao | cocoa | der Tee | tea |
| die Limonade | lemonade | das Wasser | water |
| die Milch | milk | der Wein | wine |
| der Orangensaft | orange juice | | |

## At the Restaurant

| | | | |
|---|---|---|---|
| alle sein | to not be available | die Pizzeria | pizzeria |
| Guten Appetit! | Enjoy your meal! / Tuck in! | die Selbstbedienung | self-service |
| die Diele | counter | die Serviette | serviette |
| der Gast | guest | die Speisekarte | menu |
| die Getränke | drinks | das Tagesgericht / menü | dish of the day |
| das Hauptgericht | main course | das Trinkgeld | tip |
| Herr Ober! | Waiter! | die Wurstbude | sausage stall |
| der Kunde | customer | die Vorspeise | starter |
| die Mahlzeit | meal | der Zettel | slip of paper |
| die Nachspeise / der Nachtisch | pudding / dessert | | (the bill) |

## Expressing Quantities

| | | | | |
|---|---|---|---|---|
| einige | some | ein Paar | pair |
| mehrere | several | ein Päckchen | packet |
| eine Büchse | a can | eine Packung | pack |
| eine Dose | a tin | eine Portion | portion |
| ein paar | a few | eine Schachtel | packet |
| eine Flasche | a bottle | eine Scheibe | slice |
| ein Glas | glass | ein Stück(chen) | piece |
| ein Gramm | gram | eine Tasse | cup |
| ein Kännchen | pot | eine Tüte | bag |
| ein Liter | litre | | |

You don't need a word for 'of' in German. For example:

- **Eine Portion Pommes**
  A portion *of* chips
- **Eine Tasse Tee**
  A cup *of* tea

## Quick Test

1. Say / write it in English:
   a) Ich möchte ein Butterbrot mit Pommes.
   b) Bringen Sie mir bitte die Speisekarte!
   c) Was ist das Tagesgericht?

2. Say / write it in German:
   a) I would like a bottle of lemonade please.
   b) Please bring me a packet of biscuits.
   c) A cup of tea and a bottle of mineral water.

# Food and Drink

## Useful Verbs

| | | | |
|---|---|---|---|
| *aufhören | to stop | leeren | to empty |
| backen | to bake | nehmen | to take / have |
| berühren | to stir | picknicken | to have a picnic |
| bestehen aus | to consist of | probieren | to try |
| *einnehmen | to consume | schmecken | to taste |
| essen | to eat | servieren | to serve |
| filtern | to filter | sich entscheiden | to decide |
| gern haben | to like | sich gewöhnen an | to get used to |
| | | trinken | to drink |
| *separable verb (see p.67) | | vermeiden | to avoid |

## Buying Food

| | | | |
|---|---|---|---|
| der Einkaufskorb | shopping basket | inbegriffen | included |
| die Einkaufsliste | shopping list | der Kunde / | customer |
| der Einkaufswagen | shopping trolley | die Kundin | (male / female) |
| die Eisdiele | ice cream parlour | die Quittung | receipt |
| gratis | free | der Schnellimbiss | fast food outlet |
| | | das Stehcafé | standing café |

## Eating and Drinking

| | | | |
|---|---|---|---|
| das Besteck | cutlery | der Koch | cook |
| der Dosenöffner | can opener | der Löffel | spoon |
| die Gabel | fork | das Messer | knife |
| der Gastgeber | host | der Ofen | oven |
| der Geruch | smell | das Rezept | recipe |
| das Geschirr | crockery | der Teelöffel | tea spoon |
| der Geschmack | taste | der Topf | pot |
| der Grill | barbecue | der Zucker | sugar |

## Describing What Food is Like

Here are some useful words for describing food:

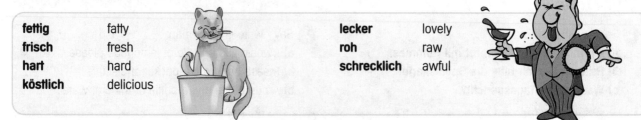

| | | | |
|---|---|---|---|
| fettig | fatty | lecker | lovely |
| frisch | fresh | roh | raw |
| hart | hard | schrecklich | awful |
| köstlich | delicious | | |

## Food and Health

| | |
|---|---|
| das Abendessen / Abendbrot | evening meal |
| ein belegtes Brot | a sandwich |
| die Energie | energy |
| der Essig | vinegar |
| das Fett | fat |
| der Fruchtsaft | fruit juice |
| das Frühstück | breakfast |
| das Mittagessen | lunch |
| die Nahrung | food |
| das Picknick | picnic |
| die Praline | praline |
| die Qualität | quality |
| die Quantität | quantity |
| der Rest | remains / leftovers |
| das Rezept | recipe |
| das Salz | salt |
| satt | full |
| die Schokolade | chocolate |
| vegetarisch | vegetarian |
| der Vegetarier | a vegetarian (male) |
| die Vegetarierin | a vegetarian (female) |

**Dieser Fruchtsaft schmeckt lecker. Was ist es eigentlich?**
This fruit juice tastes delicious. What exactly is it?

**Ich finde den Geschmack gut, aber es ist ein bisschen hart.**
I find the taste good but it is a bit hard.

**Zum Mittagessen esse ich immer eine belegtes Brot, und ich trinke eine Tasse Kaffee.**
For lunch I always have a sandwich and I drink a cup of coffee.

## Pluperfect

You already know how to form the perfect tense (see p.42).

To form the pluperfect you follow the same rules, but for the auxiliary you use the imperfect of **sein** or **haben**.
For example:

- **Ich hatte gegessen**
  I *had* eaten
- **Ich hatte gemacht**
  I *had* made
- **Ich war gegangen**
  I *had* gone

### Quick Test

1. Say / write it in English:
   a) Ich möchte die Pralinen probieren.
   b) Ich hatte um 7 Uhr Frühstück gegessen.
   c) Wir waren ins Stehcafé gegangen.
2. Say / write it in German:
   a) He avoids salt.
   b) It consists of sugar and fat.
   c) I had tried the steak. It was delicious!

# Shopping

## Shopping

|  |  |  |  |
|---|---|---|---|
| der (Zeitungs) kiosk | (newspaper) stall | das Lebensmittelgeschäft | grocery shop |
| die Bäckerei | baker's | der Markt | market |
| der Blumenladen | flower shop | die Metzgerei | butcher's |
| das Delikatessengeschäft | delicatessen | der Obst- und Gemüsehändler | greengrocer's |
| das Elektrogeschäft | electrical goods | die Parfümerie | perfume shop |
| der Fischhändler | fishmonger's | das Schmuckgeschäft | jeweller's |
| die Fleischerei | butcher's | der Supermarkt | supermarket |
| das Kleidergeschäft | clothes shop | die Süßwaren | sweets |
| die Konditorei | cake shop | das Warenhaus | department store |
| der Laden | shop | | |

## AC Prepositions

The following AC prepositions always take the Accusative Case (see p.23):

| | | | |
|---|---|---|---|
| **durch** | through | **um** | around |
| **ohne** | without | **für** | for |
| **gegen** | against | **entlang** | along |
| **wider** | against | | |

For example:
- **durch den Markt**
  through the market

## DC Prepositions

The following DC prepositions always take the *Dative Case* (see p.23):

| | | | |
|---|---|---|---|
| **aus** | out of | **nach** | after |
| **bei** | at (the house of) | **seit** | since |
| **gegenüber** | opposite | **von** | from |
| **mit** | with | **zu** | to |

For example:
- **aus dem Supermarkt**
  out of the supermarket

## AC / DC Prepositions

The following AC / DC prepositions can take either the Accusative Case or the Dative Case (see p.23):

| | |
|---|---|
| **an** | on / onto / at |
| **auf** | on |
| **unter** | under / below |
| **hinter** | behind |
| **in** | in |
| **neben** | next to / near |
| **über** | over / above |
| **vor** | in front of |
| **zwischen** | between |

You use the accusative case when you are expressing the idea of *approaching*. For example:
- **Er geht in die Konditorei**.
  He goes *into* the cake shop.
- **Wir gehen in den Supermarkt**.
  We go *Into* the supermarket.

If there isn't any idea of approaching, then you use the dative case. For example:
- **Er arbeitet in der Konditorei**.
  He works *in* the cake shop.
- **Wir kaufen alles in dem Warenhaus**.
  We buy everything *in* the department store.

## GC Prepositions

Some prepositions are followed by the Genitive Case:

| | | |
|---|---|---|
| **außerhalb** | outside | For example: |
| **innerhalb** | inside | • **trotz des Wetters** |
| **statt** | instead of | in spite of the weather |
| **trotz** | in spite of | |
| **wegen** | on account of | |

## Useful Verbs

| | | | | |
|---|---|---|---|---|
| *<u>an</u>nehmen | to accept | | passen | to fit |
| *<u>auf</u>machen | to open | | suchen | to look for |
| *<u>aus</u>geben | to spend | | unterschreiben | to sign |
| *<u>aus</u>wählen | to choose | | verkaufen | to sell |
| bedienen | to serve | | verlassen | to leave |
| bestellen | to order | | wechseln | to change |
| bezahlen | to pay for | | wiegen | to weigh |
| finden | to find | | *<u>zu</u>machen | to close |
| kaufen | to buy | | *separable verb | |

## Buying Things

| | | | | | |
|---|---|---|---|---|---|
| **Ist der Preis gut?** | Is it a good price? | **nieder** | down | **der Euro** | euro |
| **Wieviel kostet es?** | How much is it? | **die Veränderung** | change | **der Cent** | cent |
| **Wieviel bekommen Sie?** | How much do I owe you? | **die Verpackung** | packaging | **geschlossen** | shut |
| | | **der Geldschein** | bank note | **der Ruhetag** | day when closed (shop) |
| **das Sonderangebot** | a special offer | **die Münze** | coin | | |
| **der Rabatt** | discount | **das Englische Pfund** | (British) pound sterling | **beliebt** | favourite |
| **die Ermäßigung** | reduction | | | **ausverkauft** | sold out |
| **das Pfand** | deposit | **die Briefmarke** | stamp | **die Kasse** | cash till |
| **teuer** | expensive | **die Brieftasche** | wallet | **das Ding** | item / thing |
| **billig** | cheap | **das Portemonnaie** | purse | **der 10 Euroschein** | 10 euro note |
| **hoch** | high | **das Bargeld** | cash | **das 2 Eurostück** | 2 euro piece |
| **niedrig** | low | **das Kleingeld / Wechselgeld** | change | **der Schlussverkauf** | sale |
| **auf** | up | | | | |

## Quick Test

1. Say / write it in English:
   a) Ich gehe nie ins Lebensmittelgeschäft.
   b) Ich suche ein neues Portemonnaie.
   c) Der Preis ist zu hoch!

2. Say / write it in German:
   a) I often go to the department store.
   b) The electrical goods shop is very good.
   c) My brother works in the butcher's.

# Clothes and Fashion

## What to Wear

| | |
|---|---|
| der Anzug | suit |
| die Armbanduhr | watch |
| die Badehose | trunks |
| der BH (Büstenhalter) | bra |
| der Gürtel | belt |
| die Halskette | necklace |
| der Handschuh | glove |
| die Handtasche | handbag |
| das Hemd | shirt |
| die Hose | trousers |
| der Hut | hat |
| die Jacke | jacket |
| die Jeanshose | jeans |
| das Kleid | dress |
| das Kostüm | suit |
| die Krawatte | tie |
| der Mantel | coat |
| die Mütze | cap |
| der Pullover | jumper |
| der Rock | skirt |
| der Rucksack | backpack |
| der Schlafanzug | pyjamas |
| die Schuhe | shoes |
| der Slip | knickers |
| die Socken | socks |
| der Sportanzug | tracksuit |
| die Stiefel | boots |
| die Strumpfhose | tights |
| die Tätowierung | tattoo |
| die Unterhose | underpants |

**Ich suche ein Hemd aus Baumwolle.**
I'm looking for a cotton shirt.

**Haben Sie eine Krawatte aus Seide?**
Do you have a silk tie?

**Darf ich das Kleid anprobieren?**
May I try the dress on?

**Der gestreifte Rock steht dir gut.**
The striped skirt suits you well.

**Findest du die Hose ein bisschen kurz?**
Do you think the trousers are a bit short?

## Talking About Clothes

| | |
|---|---|
| (aus) Baumwolle | (made of) cotton |
| (aus) Leder | (made of) leather |
| (aus) Seide | (made of) silk |
| (aus) Wolle | (made of) wool |
| *anprobieren | to try on |
| bequem | comfortable |
| Es steht dir gut | It suits you |
| die Farbe | colour |

| | |
|---|---|
| gestreift | with stripes / striped |
| die Größe | size |
| kurz | short |
| lang | long |
| die Marke | brand |
| die Mode | fashion |
| modisch | in fashion |
| rosa | pink |
| rund | round |
| wunderbar / wunderschön | wonderful |

*separable verb (see p.67)

# Clothes and Fashion

## Demonstrative Adjectives

Demonstrative adjectives take the same endings as **der** (see p.23).

The demonstrative adjectives are...
- **dieser**  (this / these)
- **jener**  (that / those)
- **welcher?** (which? / what?)

Examples:

- **dieser Anzug**
  this suit
- **jene Jacke**
  that jacket
- **welches Kleid?**
  which dress?

**Welche Größe tragen Sie?**
What size do you wear?

**Welche Stiefel sind besser?**
Which boots are better?

**Was kosten diese Schuhe?**
What do these shoes cost?

**Diese Strumpfhose ist zu teuer.**
These tights are too expensive.

**Haben Sie diesen Mantel in Blau?**
Do you have this coat in blue?

## Adjective Endings

For adjectives after **etwas**, **viel**, **wenig** and **nichts**, you need to add a capital letter at the beginning and **-es** at the end. For example:
- **Etwas Schönes**
  Something nice
- **Nichts Interessantes**
  Nothing interesting

For adjectives after **alles**, you need to add a capital letter at the beginning and **-e** at the end. For example:
- **Alles Mögliche**
  Everything possible
- **Alles Gute!**
  All the best!

**Haben Sie etwas Billigeres?**
Do you have anything cheaper?

**Ich kann nichts Schönes finden!**
I can't find anything nice!

## Quick Test

**1** Say / write it in English:
   a) Ich trage einen schwarzen Rock und einen alten Pullover.
   b) Dieses Kleid steht dir gut.
   c) Es ist aus Seide. Es ist wunderschön.

**2** Say / write it in German:
   a) I am wearing black trousers and a white shirt.
   b) These boots are too small.
   c) This jacket is too short.

# Practice Questions

## Reading

**1** The following statements are reasons for and against smoking.
Put each statement into the correct column in the table.

| für das Rauchen | gegen das Rauchen |
| --- | --- |
| | |
| | |
| | |
| | |
| | |
| | |

**A**   Man kann Lungenkrebs bekommen.

**B**   Die Kleider und die Haare riechen.

**C**   Man kann sich entspannen, wenn man mit Freunden ist.

**D**   Die Zähne werden braun.

**E**   Das kostet sehr viel Geld.

**F**   Alle meine Freunde rauchen, deswegen will ich auch rauchen.

**G**   Das ist eine Geldverschwendung.

**H**   Ich mag den Geschmack nicht.

**2** Read what these people say about their eating habits and then answer, in English, the questions that follow.

**Ich esse nie Frühstück. Zu Mittag gehe ich in die Schulkantine. Ich esse jeden Tage nur einen grünen Salat mit Jogurt. Ich esse zu Abend mit meinen Eltern zu Hause. Ich esse nie Fleisch und nie Fisch.**

Dörte

**Ich esse Haferflocken zum Frühstück und ich trinke normalerweise Kaffee. Zu Mittag esse ich immer mit meiner Mutter und meiner kleinen Schwester zu Hause. Zum Abendbrot essen wir normalerweise Wurst oder Käse.**

Jennifer

**Zum Frühstück esse ich gewöhnlich Toastbrote mit Honig und ich trinke Orangensaft. Das ist um halb sieben. In der Mittagspause esse ich mit Freunden in der Schulkantine. Das Essen ist köstlich aber ein bisschen teuer. Mein Lieblingsessen ist Steak mit Pommes.**

Patrick

**a)** Who doesn't eat breakfast? ....................

**b)** Who doesn't eat in the school canteen? ....................

**c)** Who has coffee at breakfast time? ....................

**d)** Who eats honey? ....................

**e)** Who could be a vegetarian? ....................

**f)** Who eats breakfast at 6.30? ....................

## Speaking

**3** Give a full response, in German, to each of the questions below. Say your answer out loud.

**a)** Was isst du gern?

**b)** Rauchst du? Warum oder warum nicht?

**c)** Trinkst du Alkohol? Warum oder warum nicht?

**d)** Was machst du, um fit zu bleiben?

**e)** Gehst du gern einkaufen?

**f)** Was für Kleider trägst du gern?

**g)** Du kaufst Geschenke fur deine Freunde und Freundinnen. Was kaufst du?

## Writing

**4** You are writing an account about your lifestyle. Write about each of the following, in German.

**a)** Describe the sport that you do or what you do in order to keep fit.

**b)** Describe what kind of food and drink you normally consume.

**c)** Explain why it is important to stay fit and healthy.

**5** Write about a recent shopping trip you've been on.

**a)** Say which shops you went to and who you went with.

**b)** Say what you bought and what else you did during the trip.

**c)** Say what you liked / disliked about the day, and what you would do differently next time.

# Leisure and Pastimes

## Talking About Your Spare Time

| | | | |
|---|---|---|---|
| angeln | to go fishing | der Verein | club |
| E-mails schicken | to send emails | die Volksmusik | folk music |
| in den Jugendclub gehen | to go to the youth club | die Vorstellung | performance |
| in einem Chor singen | to sing in a choir | zum Fußballspiel gehen | to go to a football match |
| (zum) Bowling gehen | to go bowling | | |
| die (Blas)kapelle | (brass) band | Ich interessiere mich für… | I am interested in… |
| ins Kino gehen | to go to the cinema | Ich habe kein Interesse an… | I'm not interested in… |
| ins Konzert gehen | to go to a concert | Ich habe die Nase voll von… | I'm sick of… |
| ins Theater gehen | to go to the theatre | | |
| klassische Musik | classical music | | |
| meine Lieblingsband | my favourite band | | |
| Musik hören | to listen to music | | |
| die Popmusik | pop music | | |
| die Rockmusik | rock music | | |
| Rollschuh laufen | to go roller skating | | |
| rudern | to row | | |
| Schach spielen | to play chess | | |
| schreiben | to write | | |
| das Snowboarden | snowboarding | | |
| surfen | to surf the internet | | |
| tanzen | to dance | | |
| die Theatergruppe | drama group | | |
| üben | to practise | | |

## Adverbial Phrases

Here are some useful phrases you can use to make your language more interesting:

| | |
|---|---|
| ab und zu | from time to time |
| im Allgemeinen | generally |
| im Großen und Ganzen | generally |
| immer noch | still |
| jeden Abend | every evening |
| jeden Tag | every day |
| noch einmal | once again |
| ohne Pause | without stopping |
| zu Hause | at home |

# Leisure and Pastimes

## At the Cinema

**Ich sehe (nicht) gern…**
I (don't) like to watch…

**Ich interessiere mich für…**
I am interested in…

| | |
|---|---|
| **Abenteuerfilme** | adventure films |
| **historische Filme** | historical films |
| **Horrorfilme** | horror films |
| **Komödien** | comedies |
| **Krimis** | thrillers |
| **Liebesfilme** | love stories |
| **romantische Filme** | romantic films |
| **Science-Fiction Filme** | science fiction films |
| **Zeichentrickfilme** | cartoons |

## Talking About Films

| | |
|---|---|
| **die Begeisterung** | enthusiasm |
| **der Beginn** | beginning |
| **der Blödsinn!** | rubbish! |
| **der Charakter** | character |
| **das Eintrittsgeld** | price of ticket |
| **die Eintrittskarte** | ticket |
| **empfehlen** | to recommend |

| | |
|---|---|
| **herrlich** | excellent |
| **hervorragend** | superb |
| **das Ende** | ending |
| **meinen / denken** | to think |
| **neu** | new |
| **neulich** | recently |
| **sich freuen auf** | to look forward to |

## Using Adjectives

You already know the adjective endings to use after **der** and **ein**, etc. (see p.24).

If there is no other word before the noun (e.g. 'the' or 'my') use the following endings:

| | Masculine | Feminine | Neuter | Plural |
|---|---|---|---|---|
| **Nominative** | -er | -e | -es | -e |
| **Accusative** | -en | -e | -es | -e |
| **Genitive** | -en | -er | -en | -er |
| **Dative** | -em | -er | -em | -en |

For example:
- **romantische Filme** (plural)
- **klassische Musik** (feminine singular)

### Quick Test

1. Say / write it in English:
   a) Ich singe in einem Chor.
   b) Ich gehe ab und zu ins Konzert.
   c) Ich sehe nicht gern Liebesfilme.
   d) Ich interessiere mich nicht für klassische Musik.
2. Say / write it in German:
   a) I like to watch horror films and adventure films.
   b) I do not go to the cinema often.
   c) In general we like pop music and rock music.
   d) I'm sick of old science fiction films.

# Leisure and Pastimes

## Useful Verbs

| | |
|---|---|
| *<u>an</u>fangen | to start |
| buchen | to book |
| *<u>ein</u>laden | to invite |
| hoffen | to hope |
| holen | to fetch |
| hören | to hear |
| kommen | to come |
| reservieren | to reserve |
| sich entspannen | to relax |
| sich freuen über | to be pleased about |
| spenden | to donate / pay for someone |
| sich treffen mit | to meet up with |
| *<u>zurück</u>rufen | to call back |

*separable verb (see p.67)

## Other Expressions

| | |
|---|---|
| die Einladung | invitation |
| günstig | convenient |
| heute | today |
| Klasse! | great! |
| der Kontakt | contact |
| lieb | dear |
| morgen (früh) | tomorrow (morning) |
| nicht mehr | no longer |
| nicht nur…, sondern auch | not only…, but also |
| prima! | great! |
| schließlich | finally |
| am Wochenende | at the weekend |
| wohin? | where to? |
| die Zeit | time |
| zuerst | first |
| zufällig | by any chance |

Remember, if you use a verb that needs an infinitive, the infinitive goes to the end of the sentence. For example:

- **Ich werde zwei Plätze buchen.**
  I will book two seats.
- **Möchtest du zufällig ins Konzert kommen?**
  Would you by any chance like to come to the concert?

# Leisure and Pastimes

## Reading

| | |
|---|---|
| **der Artikel** | the article |
| **das Buch** | the book |
| **das Komikheft** | the comic |
| **der Roman** | the novel |
| **die Zeitschrift** | the magazine |

**Ich lese gern Zeitschriften und Komikhefte.**
I like reading magazines and comics.

**Ich mag historische Romane und Bücher über andere Länder.**
I like historical novels and books about other countries.

## Playing Musical Instruments

| | | | | |
|---|---|---|---|---|
| **die Blockflöte** | flute | | **die Melodie** | melody |
| **die Flöte** | flute | | **die Oboe** | oboe |
| **die Geige** | violin | | **das Orchester** | orchestra |
| **die Gitarre** | guitar | | **das Saxophon** | saxophone |
| **das Keyboard** | keyboard | | **das Schlagzeug** | drums |
| **die Klarinette** | clarinet | | **die Trompete** | trumpet |
| **das Klavier** | piano | | | |

## Saying 'How Long For'

To say how long you have been doing something for, or how long something has been going on for, you can use **seit** with the present tense:

- **Ich spiele seit drei Jahren Flöte.**
  I've been playing the flute *for three years*.
- **Ich lerne seit zwei Jahren Deutsch.**
  I've been learning German *for two years*.

Remember, **seit** takes the dative (see p.54).

## Quick Test

1. Say / write it in English:
   a) Ich spiele seit einem Jahr Geige.
   b) Möchtest du am Wochenende ins Rockmusikkonzert kommen?
   c) Ich spiele Gitarre, um mich zu entspannen.

2. Say / write it in German:
   a) Would you like to come to the cinema? Yes, great!
   b) I have been playing the drums for five years.
   c) I don't like listening to classical music. It's rubbish!

63

# Events and Celebrations

## Celebrations

| | | | |
|---|---|---|---|
| **Wann ist das?** | When is it? | **die Geschenke** | presents |
| **im Frühling** | in Spring | **die Hochzeit** | wedding |
| **im Sommer** | in Summer | **die Karte** | card |
| **im Herbst** | in Autumn | **die Kerzen** | candles |
| **im Winter** | in Winter | **die Lichter** | lights |
| **im März / Oktober** | in March / October | **die Lieder** | songs |
| | | **die (silberne) Hochzeit** | (Silver) Anniversary |
| **die Feier** | party | **der Tanz** | dance |
| **der Feiertag** | public holiday | **die Taufe** | christening |
| **das Fest** | festival | **der Tod** | death |
| **das Feuerwerk** | firework display | **der Umzug** | procession |
| **die Geburt** | birth | **die Verlobung** | engagement |
| **der Geburtstag** | birthday | | |

## Special Holidays

| | |
|---|---|
| **der Heiligabend** | Christmas Eve |
| **Karneval / Fasching** | carnival (February) |
| **Ostern** | Easter |
| **Pfingsten** | Whitsun |
| **Silvester** | New Year |
| **der Weihnachtsmann** | Father Christmas |
| **Weihnachten** | Christmas |

## Useful Verbs

| | |  | | |
|---|---|---|---|---|
| **anziehen** | to put on | | **geben** | to give |
| **anzünden** | to light | | **schicken** | to send |
| **bekommen** | to receive | | **schmücken** | to decorate |
| **bestehen...aus** | to consist of | | **singen** | to sing |
| **essen** | to eat | | **tanzen** | to dance |
| **feiern** | to celebrate | | **trinken** | to drink |
| | | | **warten auf** | to wait for |
| *separable verb (see p.67) | | | **wünschen** | to wish |

## Useful Things to Say

| | |
|---|---|
| **fröhliche Weihnachten!** | Happy Christmas |
| **Ich gratuliere!** | Congratulations! |
| **Herzlichen Glückwunsch zum Geburtstag!** | Happy birthday! |
| **Prost!** | Cheers! |

# Events and Celebrations

## Pronouns – Cases

Make sure you know the different cases for the pronouns:

| Pronoun | Nominatve | Accusative | Dative |
|---------|-----------|------------|--------|
| I, me | ich | mich | mir |
| you | du | dich | dir |
| he / him | er | ihn | ihm |
| she / her | sie | sie | ihr |
| it | es | es | ihm |
| we / us | wir | uns | uns |
| you | ihr | euch | euch |
| you | Sie | Sie | Ihnen |

To remind yourself how to use the different cases, refer back to p.23.

For example:
- **Sie laden** mich **zur Hochzeitsfeier ein**.
  They are inviting me to the wedding celebration.
- **Ich tanze gern** mit ihr.
  I like to dance *with her*.

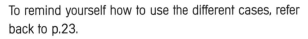

## The 'damit' Rule

You can join **da-** to the front of a preposition to mean '… it'. For example:
- **damit**     with it
- **dafür**     for it
- **davon**     from it

## The 'womit' Rule

You can join **wo-** to the front of a preposition to mean '… what' or '… which'. For example:
- **Womit zahlst du?**     With what are you paying?
- **Woraus besteht es?**   Of what (literally 'out of what') does it consist?

## Dative Plural

When you use the dative plural, you need to add **-n** to every noun and pronoun. For example:
- **Ich spiele mit meinen Freunden und Freundinnen.**
  I play with my friends (male and female).

## Quick Test

**1** Say / write it in English:
  a) **Zu Weihnachten bekommen wir Karten.**
  b) **Wir haben Kerzen, und wir singen Weihnachtslieder.**
  c) **Wir schmücken den Weihnachtsbaum.**

**2** Say / write it in German:
  a) I like to celebrate my birthday.
  b) We went to the Christmas market in December.
  c) Their engagement was in Spring.

# Sport and Exercise

## Sports

For many sports you can use the infinitive of the verb as a noun.

The following are all neuter (**das**):

| | |
|---|---|
| **Angeln** | fishing |
| **Eislaufen** | skating |
| **Joggen** | running |
| **Kegeln** | bowling |
| **Klettern** | climbing |
| **Radfahren** | cycling |
| **Reiten** | riding |
| **Rollschuhlaufen** | roller-skating |
| **Schlittschuhlaufen** | ice-skating |
| **Schwimmen** | swimming |
| **Skateboard fahren** | skate-boarding |
| **Spazierengehen** | go for a walk |
| **Tanzen** | dancing |
| **Wasserskilaufen** | waterskiing |
| **Windsurfen** | windsurfing |

## Other Useful Words

| | | | | |
|---|---|---|---|---|
| **das Aerobic** | aerobics | | **spielen** | to play |
| **aktiv** | active | | **der Spieler** | player |
| **das Badminton** | badminton | | **der Spielplatz** | playground |
| **der Basketball** | basketball | | **sportlich** | sporty |
| **draußen** | outdoors | | **der Sportplatz** | sports ground / pitch |
| **drinnen** | indoors | | **der Tanz** | dance |
| **die Freizeit** | leisure time | | **die Teilnahme** | participation |
| **der Fußball** | football | | **der Tennis** | tennis |
| **der Golf** | golf | | **der Tischtennis** | table tennis |
| **die Gymnastik** | gymnastics | | **trainieren** | to train |
| **der Handball** | handball | | **die Übung** | practice |
| **der Klub** | club | | **wandern** | to hike |
| **die Leichtathletik** | athletics | | **die Wanderungen** | walks / hikes |
| **die Spaziergänge** | walks (short) | | | |

To talk about your favourite activity, you can simply join **Lieblings-** to the front of any noun. For example:

- **Fußball ist mein Lieblingsspiel.**
  Football is my favourite game.

# Sport and Exercise

## More About Using 'Seit'

You can use **seit** with the imperfect tense to say how long you had been doing something. For example:

- **Wir hatten seit zwei Stunden Tischtennis gespielt.**
  We had been playing table tennis *for two hours*.

Remember, seit takes the dative (see p.54).

## Sports – Useful words

| | | | |
|---|---|---|---|
| **der Gewinn** | the win | ***teilnehmen** | to take part |
| **gewinnen** | to win | **das Tor** | goal |
| **die Mannschaft** | team | **verlieren** | to lose |
| **das Mitglied** | member | **der Verlust** | a loss |
| | | *separable verb* | |

## Useful Verbs

| | | | |
|---|---|---|---|
| ***abfahren** | to set off | ***umsteigen** | to change |
| ***absteigen** | to get off | **warten** | to wait |
| ***ankommen** | to arrive | ***zurückfahren** | to drive back |
| ***aufstehen** | to stand up | ***zurückgehen** | to go back |
| ***einsteigen** | to get on | ***zurückkommen** | to come back |
| **fahren** | to travel | | |
| **sich *hinsetzen** | to sit down | *separable verb* | |

## Separable Verbs

You can recognise separable verbs because they start with a *separable prefix*, e.g. **ab-, an-, auf-, aus-, ein-, fern-, fort-, her-, herunter-, hin-, hoch-, mit-, nach-, teil-, um-, vor-, weg-, weiter-, zu-, zurück-, zusammen-**:

You need to send the separable prefix to the end of the sentence, for example:

- **Nach dem Spiel gehen wir nach Hause zurück.**
  After the game we go back home.

*N.B. In this book you can recognise the separable verbs because the separable prefix is underlined.*

## Quick Test

**1** Say / write it in English:
  a) Handball ist mein Lieblingsspiel.
  b) Ich mache sehr gern Wanderungen in den Bergen.
  c) Wasserskilaufen finde ich toll!

**2** Say / write it in German:
  a) I like to windsurf.
  b) I find gymnastics very interesting.
  c) Where is the playground?

# Media Entertainment

## Television

| | | | |
|---|---|---|---|
| **Was läuft im Fernsehen?** | What's on TV? | **funktionieren** | to work |
| **eine Gameshow** | game show | **HD** | HD (high definition) |
| **eine Kindersendung** | children's programme | **das Kabelfernsehen** | cable TV |
| **eine Musiksendung** | music programme | **die Kamera** | camera |
| **eine Spielsendung** | game show | **der Krimi** | detective programme |
| **eine Sportsendung** | sports programme | **die Nachrichten** | news |
| **eine Talkshow** | talk show | **das Programm** | channel |
| **der Zeichentrickfilm** | cartoon | **das Satellitenfernsehen** | satellite TV |
| | | **die Seifenoper** | soap |
| **am Apparat** | speaking (on the phone) | **die Serie** | series |
| **der Bildschirm** | screen | **das Videogerät** | video machine |
| **digital** | digital | **die Werbung** | adverts |
| **der Dokumentarfilm** | documentary | **der Wetterbericht** | weather forecast / report |
| **elektrisch** | electrical | **die Wettervorhersage** | weather forecast |
| **das Fernsehgerät** | TV set | | |

## Useful Verbs

| | | | | | |
|---|---|---|---|---|---|
| *<u>an</u>machen | to turn on | *<u>aus</u>schalten | to switch off | **senden** | to broadcast |
| *<u>an</u>rufen | to call | *<u>ein</u>schalten | to switch on | **telefonieren** | to phone |
| *<u>an</u>sehen | to watch | *<u>herunter</u>laden | to download | **zuhören** | to listen to |
| *<u>auf</u>nehmen | to record | *<u>hoch</u>laden | to upload | | |
| *<u>aus</u>machen | to turn off | **schicken** | to send | *separable verb (see p.67) | |

## Relative Pronouns

Relative pronouns relate back to someone or something you have already mentioned in a sentence. In English they translate as 'which' or 'who'.

- Use **der** to refer back to a masculine subject.
- Use **die** to refer back to a feminine subject.
- Use **das** to refer back to a neuter subject.
- Use **die** to refer back to a plural subject.

For example:

- **Der Wetterbericht, der gestern im Fernsehen war, war nicht gut.**
  The weather report, *which* was on the TV yesterday, was not good.
- **Die Sendung, die wir gesehen haben, war langweilig.**
  The programme, *which* we watched, was boring.
- **Das Buch, das ich gelesen habe, war toll!**
  The book, *which* I read, was great!
- **Die Sendungen, die für Kinder sind, sind doof!**
  The programmes, *which* are for children, are stupid!

When you use a relative pronoun, you have to send the verb to the end of the sentence.

Make sure you don't muddle up the relative pronouns with the various words for 'the'.

## Computers and Internet Communication

| | | | | | |
|---|---|---|---|---|---|
| **chatten** | to chat | **das Handy** | mobile (phone) | **der Schrägstrich** | forward slash |
| **clicken** | to click | **der iPod** | iPod | **die Tastatur** | keyboard |
| **der Computer** | computer | **der Vertrag** | contract | **der Drucker** | printer |
| **das Fax** | fax | **die Batterie** | battery | **kopieren** | to copy |
| **das Gewicht** | the weight | **die CD** | CD | **kostenlos** | free |
| **das Kennwort** | password | **die E-Mail** | email | **löschen** | to delete |
| **das MP3** | MP3 | **die Maus** | mouse | **programmieren** | to programme |
| **der Fotoapparat** | camera | **die Rechnung** | bill | | |

## Other Methods of Communication

| | | | | | |
|---|---|---|---|---|---|
| **die Adresse** | address | **das Foto** | photograph | **das Mittel** | means |
| **die Anzeige** | notice | **fotografieren** | to photograph | (e.g. **Kommunikationsmittel** – | |
| **das Bild** | picture | **\*mitteilen** | to communicate | means of communication) | |
| **der Brief** | letter | | | **das Plakat** | poster |
| **die Brieffreund(in)** | pen friend | *separable verb (see p.67)* | | **die Stereoanlage** | stereo system |

## More About Relative Pronouns

On p.68 you revised relative pronouns in the nominative case. But, you can also use relative pronouns in the other cases. The forms are shown in the following table:

| Relative Pronoun | Masculine | Feminine | Neuter | Plural |
|---|---|---|---|---|
| Accusative | den | die | das | die |
| Genitive | dessen | deren | dessen | deren |
| Dative | dem | der | dem | denen |

For example:
- **Der Drucker, den ich benutze.** (masculine accusative)
  The printer which I use.
- **Die Leute, mit denen ich arbeite.** (dative plural)
  The people with whom I work.
- **Wessen?**
  Whose?
- **Wessen Computer ist das?**
  Whose computer is that?

If the relative pronoun relates back to an *entire clause* rather than one specific item, you would use **was** as the relative pronoun:
- **Die Musik ist zu laut, was meine Mutter sehr unangenehm findet.**
  The music is too loud, which my mother finds unpleasant.

### Quick Test

1. Say / write it in English:
   a) **Ich sehe sehr gern Seifenoper.**
   b) **Meine Mutter sieht sehr gern Sportsendungen.**
   c) **Unser Fernsehgerät funktioniert nicht.**
2. Say / write it in German:
   a) Can I record the programme?
   b) I like to watch music programmes.
   c) I never watch the news.

# Practice Questions

## Reading

**1** Read the passages below and answer, in English, the questions that follow.

Ich lese furchtbar gern. Ich gehe zweimal in der Woche in die Bibliothek. Ich lese alles Mögliche – Liebesromane, Zeitschriften, Komikhefte. Science Fiction aber finde ich doof!

Ursula

Ich bin Mitglied eines Tennisklubs. Ich hoffe, als Geburtstagsgeschenk einen neuen Tennisschläger zu bekommen.

Richard

Wir wohnen auf dem Lande, und ich habe mein eigenes Pferd. Am Wochenende gehe ich reiten.

Anna

Am Wochenende gehe ich sehr gern mit meinen Freunden ins Freibad. Das macht Spaß und ist auch gesund.

Manuel

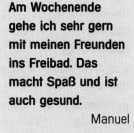

**a)** Who goes horse riding? _____

**b)** Who goes swimming? _____

**c)** Who goes to the library? _____

**d)** Why does Richard mention his birthday? _____

**e)** Who finds their pastime healthy? _____

**f)** What doesn't Ursula like? _____

**2** Read the descriptions of three celebrations below and answer the questions that follow.

Zu Ostern werden wir nach Spanien fliegen. Man wird sich sonnen, schwimmen und sich entspannen. Ich werde auch viele Bücher lesen. Ich kann kaum warten!

Beate

Mein Geburtstag ist im Mai. Dieses Jahr gehe ich mit meiner Familie ins Konzert. Ich freue mich darauf.

Ahmed

Zu Weihnachten war meine Familie zusammen. Auch mein Bruder war da, der in Italien wohnt. Wir haben zuviel gegessen und getrunken, aber ich habe ein paar tolle Geschenke für meine Geschwister gekauft.

Nora

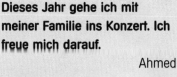

**a)** Who wrote in the past tense? _____

**b)** Who wrote in the present tense? _____

**c)** Who wrote in the future tense? _____

## Speaking

**3** Give a full response, in German, to each of the questions below. Say your answer out loud.

**a)** Was machst du gern am Wochenende?

**b)** Was hast du letztes Wochenende gemacht?

**c)** Was möchtest du in den nächsten Ferien machen?

**d)** Gehst du oft ins Kino? Hast du einen Lieblingsschauspieler oder Schauspielerin?

## Writing

**4** You are describing your last birthday party. Write about each of the following, in German.

**a)** Explain what you did and who came to your party.

**b)** Describe the presents that you got and what you thought of them.

**c)** Describe how you would like to celebrate your next birthday.

**5** You are writing about your plans for a day out at the seaside /countryside. Write about each of the following, in German.

**a)** Say how you're going to get there.

**b)** Say what you're hoping to do during the day and why.

**c)** Describe what happened on your last visit to the seaside / countryside.

# Holidays and Travelling

## Countries Around the World

Remember to use **nach** to say *to* a country and **in** for *in* the country.

- **Ich fahre nach Deutschland.**    I am going *to* Germany.
- **Ich wohne in England.**    I live *in* England.

| | | | |
|---|---|---|---|
| **Afrika** | Africa | **Irland** | Ireland |
| **Amerika** | America | **Italien** | Italy |
| **Asien** | Asia | **Japan** | Japan |
| **Australien** | Australia | **die Niederlande**\*\* | Netherlands |
| **Belgien** | Belgium | **Österreich** | Austria |
| **China** | China | **Pakistan** | Pakistan |
| **Dänemark** | Denmark | **Polen** | Poland |
| **Deutschland** | Germany | **Portugal** | Portugal |
| **England** | England | **Russland** | Russia |
| **Europa** | Europe | **Schottland** | Scotland |
| **Frankreich** | Portugal | **die Schweiz**\* | Switzerland |
| **Griechenland** | Greece | **Spanien** | Spain |
| **Großbritannien** | Great Britain | **die Türkei**\* | Turkey |
| **Holland** | Holland | **die Vereinigten Staaten**\*\* | USA |
| **Indien** | India | **Wales** | Wales |

\*These countries are *feminine*, so you use **in die** for 'to' and **in der** for 'in'. For example:
- **Ich fahre in die Schweiz.**
  I am going to Switzerland.
- **Er wohnt in der Türkei.**
  He lives in Turkey.

\*\*These countries are *plural*, so you use **in die** for 'to' and **in den** for 'in'. For example:
- **Ich fahre in die Niederlande.**
  I am going to the Netherlands.
- **Er arbeitet in den Vereinigten Staaten.**
  He works in the USA.

## Know Your Geography

| | | | | | |
|---|---|---|---|---|---|
| **der Ärmelkanal** | English Channel | **Köln** | Cologne | **die Ostsee** | Baltic Sea |
| **Bayern** | Bavaria | **das Mittelmeer** | Mediterranean | **der Rhein** | Rhine |
| **der Bodensee** | Lake Constance | **die Mosel** | the Moselle | **der Schwarzwald** | Black Forest |
| **die Donau** | the Danube | **München** | Munich | **der Tunnel** | Channel Tunnel |
| **Genf** | Geneva | **die Nordsee** | North Sea | **Wien** | Vienna |

## Where to Stay on Holiday

| | | | |
|---|---|---|---|
| **an der Küste** | on the coast | **in einer Ferienwohnung** | in a holiday apartment |
| **auf dem Lande** | in the country | **in einem Hotel** | in a hotel |
| **auf einem Campingplatz** | on a campsite | **in einem Wohnwagen** | in a caravan |
| **im Gebirge** | in the mountains | **in einer Jugendherberge** | in a youth hostel |
| **in einem Ferienhaus** | in a holiday cottage | **in einer Stadt** | in a city |

## Travelling About

| | | | | | |
|---|---|---|---|---|---|
| **auf einem Pferd** | on horseback | **mit dem Flugzeug** | by plane | **mit dem Zug** | by train |
| **mit dem (Segel)boot** | by (sailing) boat | **mit dem Mofa** | by moped | **mit der Straßenbahn** | by tram |
| **mit dem Auto / Wagen** | by car | **mit dem Motorrad** | by motorbike | **zu Fuß** | on foot |
| **mit dem Bus** | by bus / coach | **mit dem Schiff** | by ship / boat | **zweiter Klasse** | second class |
| **mit dem Fahrrad** | by bike | **mit dem Taxi** | by taxi | | |

## Nationalities / Adjectives

| Male | Female | Plural | Adjective | Meaning |
|------|--------|--------|-----------|---------|
| der Afrikaner | die Afrikanerin | die Afrikaner | afrikanisch | African |
| der Belgier | die Belgierin | die Belgier | belgisch | Belgian |
| der Brite | die Britin | die Briten | british | British |
| der Chinese | die Chinesin | die Chinesen | chinesisch | Chinese |
| der Däne | die Dänin | die Dänen | dänisch | Danish |
| der Deutsche | die Deutsche | die Deutschen | deutsch | German |
| der Engländer | die Engländerin | die Engländer | englisch | English |
| der Franzose | die Französin | die Franzosen | französisch | French |
| der Grieche | die Griechin | die Griechen | griechisch | Greek |
| der Holländer | die Holländerin | die Holländer | holländisch | Dutch |
| der Inder | die Inderin | die Inder | indisch | Indian |
| der Ire | die Irin | die Iren | irisch | Irish |
| der Italiener | die Italienerin | die Italiener | italienisch | Italian |
| der Japaner | die Japanerin | die Japaner | japanisch | Japanese |
| der Kanadier | die Kanadierin | die Kanadier | kanadisch | Canadian |
| der Österreicher | die Österreicherin | die Österreicher | österreichisch | Austrian |
| der Pakistaner | die Pakistanerin | die Pakistaner | pakistanisch | Pakistani |
| der Portugiese | die Portugiesin | die Portugiesen | portugiesisch | Portuguese |
| der Russe | die Russin | die Russen | russisch | Russian |
| der Schotte | die Schottin | die Schotten | schottisch | Scottish |
| der Schweizer | die Schweizerin | die Schweizer | schweizerisch | Swiss |
| der Spanier | die Spanierin | die Spanier | spanisch | Spanish |
| der Walise | die Walisin | die Walisen | walisisch | Welsh |

## Useful Expressions and Verbs

| | |
|---|---|
| nach Hause | (going) home |
| zu Hause | at home |
| *abfahren | to set off |
| begleiten | to accompany |
| besuchen | to visit |
| fahren | to travel |
| kaufen | to buy |
| mieten | to hire |
| schreiben | to write |

| | |
|---|---|
| schwimmen | to swim |
| segeln | to sail |
| sich *ausruhen | to rest |
| sich sonnen | to sunbathe |
| vergessen | to forget |

*separable verb (see p.67)

### Quick Test

1. Say / write it in English:
   a) Ich fahre sehr gern nach Österreich
   b) Wir fahren jedes Jahr nach Köln.
   c) Normalerweise bleiben wir im Wohnwagen.
2. Say / write it in German:
   a) We travel by coach.
   b) We are staying in a holiday cottage.
   c) Munich is not by the sea.

# Holidays and Travelling

## Describing Your Holiday

**Ich bin nach Wien in Österreich gefahren.**
I went to Vienna in Austria.

**Ich habe im Juli zwei Wochen in Wien verbracht.**
I spent two weeks in Vienna in July.

**Ich bin mit meinen Freunden und Freundinnen gefahren.**
I went with my friends.

**Wir sind geflogen.**
We flew.

## Using the Imperfect Tense

You can translate the imperfect tense as 'I did' something, 'I was doing' something, or 'I used to do' something. For example:

- **Ich spielte Geige**.    I used to play the violin.
- **Wir wohnten in London**.    We lived in London.

You mainly meet the imperfect tense in writing, not in speech.

To form the imperfect, first decide whether the verb is strong or weak.

## Imperfect – Strong Verbs

Look in the strong verb list on p.88–89, or a dictionary, to find out if a verb is strong. Then find the 'imperfect', and add these endings:

| | |
|---|---|
| **ich** (no ending) | **ihr** -t |
| **du** -st | **sie** -en |
| **er / sie / es** (no ending) | **Sie** -en |
| **wir** -en | |

Examples:
- **fahren** ➡ **ich** fuhr    I went
- **bleiben** ➡ **wir** blieben    we stayed
- **fliegen** ➡ **er** flog    he flew

## Imperfect – Weak Verbs

When you have a weak verb...
- take the infinitive and knock off the final -en
- add the endings shown here.

| | |
|---|---|
| **ich** -te | **ihr** -tet |
| **du** -test | **sie** -ten |
| **er / sie / es** -te | **Sie** -ten |
| **wir** -ten | |

Examples:
- **machen** ➡ **ich** machte    I made
- **kaufen** ➡ **er** kaufte    he bought
- **sagen** ➡ **sie** sagten    they said

Remember, if a verb is not in the strong verb list (p.88–89) assume it is weak.

## Getting Around

| | | | | |
|---|---|---|---|---|
| **die Autobahn** | motorway | | **der Hafen** | port |
| **der Bahnhof** | station | | **der Pass** | passport |
| **der Bahnsteig** | platform | | **die S-Bahn** | suburban railway |
| **der D-Zug / ICE** | fast train | | **das Schließfach** | locker |
| **der Eingang** | entrance | | **der Speisewagen** | buffet car |
| **die Fähre** | ferry | | **die Straße** | road |
| **die Fahrkarte** | ticket | | **tanken** | to put fuel in |
| **der Fahrkartenschalter** | ticket office | | **die Tankstelle** | petrol station |
| **der Flughafen** | airport | | | |

## Useful Words

| | | | |
|---|---|---|---|
| **die Abfahrt** | departure | **der Notausgang** | emergency exit |
| **die Ankunft** | arrival | **öffentlich** | public |
| **der Ausgang** | exit | **pünktlich** | on time |
| **der Fahrradverleih** | bike hire | **die Rundfahrt** | round trip |
| **drucken** | to push | **der See** | lake |
| **fliegen** | to fly | **die Sehenswürdigkeiten** | the sights |
| **früh** | early | **der Sitz** | seat |
| **die Führung** | conducted tour | **der Stadtbummel** | tour of town |
| **der Kilometer** | kilometre | **die Überfahrt** | crossing |
| **langsam** | slow | **unterwegs** | en route |
| **die Meile** | mile | **verspätet** | late |
| **\*mitkommen /\*mitgehen** | to accompany | **ziehen** | to pull |
| **\*mitnehmen** | to take with you | **der Zoll** | customs |

*\*separable verb (see p.67)*

## Next Year's Holiday

**Wie sind deine idealen Ferien?**
What's your ideal holiday?

**Ich möchte in den Vereinigten Staaten fahren.**
I'd like to go to the USA.

**Ich will dort einen Monat verbringen.**
I want to spend a month there.

**Ich werde mit meinen Freunden fahren, weil es Spaß macht.**
I'll go with my friends because it's fun.

**Wir werden mit dem Flugzeug fliegen und in einem Luxushotel bleiben.**
We'll travel by plane and stay in a luxury hotel.

**Ich will in den Warenhäusern von New York einkaufen gehen.**
I want to go shopping in the department stores in New York.

Remember, you don't need a word for 'for' when talking about 'how long'. For example:

- **Wir sind zwei Wochen geblieben.**
  We stayed (for) two weeks.
- **Ich war eine Woche in Berlin.**
  I was in Berlin for a week.

### Quick Test

1. Say / write it in English:
   a) **Ich war drei Wochen in Spanien.**
   b) **Wir haben eine Stadtführung gemacht.**
   c) **Die Überfahrt war sehr gut.**
2. Say / write it in German:
   a) We stayed in Portugal for one week.
   b) I like to travel by boat.
   c) Where is the emergency exit?

# Holidays and Accommodation

## Organising Accommodation

| | | |
|---|---|---|
| im Erdgeschoss | on the ground floor | |
| im ersten Stock | on the first floor | |
| auf der zweiten Etage | on the second floor | |
| das Doppelzimmer | double room | |
| das Einzelzimmer | single room | |

| | |
|---|---|
| die Halbpension | half board |
| das Mehrbettzimmer | family room |
| die Nacht | the night |
| die Unterkunft | accommodation |
| die Vollpension | full board |

## Facilities in Your Room

| | |
|---|---|
| das Badezimmer | bathroom |
| das Doppelbett | double bed |
| das Haarwaschmittel | shampoo |
| das Handtuch | towel |
| die Seife | soap |

| | |
|---|---|
| der Spiegel | mirror |
| die Steppdecke | quilt |
| das Waschbecken | wash-basin |
| der Wasserhahn | tap |
| der Wecker | alarm clock |

## Other Useful Words and Expressions

| | |
|---|---|
| der Aufzug | lift |
| die Aussicht | the view |
| das Bett | bed |
| die Broschüre | brochure |
| der Empfang | reception |
| das Formular | form |
| das Hotelverzeichnis | hotel list |
| die Miete | rent |
| im Voraus | in advance |
| mit Blick auf… | with a view of… |
| das Prospekt | brochure |
| die Rechnung | the bill |
| die Rezeption | reception |
| die Rolltreppe | escalator |
| der Schlüssel | key |
| die Seife | soap |
| das Stock(werk) | floor / storey |
| die Treppe | stairs |
| das Treppenhaus | stairs |
| die Übernachtung | overnight stay |

**Ich möchte ein Zimmer für zwei Nächte reservieren.**
I'd like to reserve a room for two nights.

**Ich hätte gern ein Doppelzimmer mit Dusche und mit einem Blick auf das Meer.**
I would like a double room with a shower and a sea view.

**Ich habe eine Reservieung für zwei im Namen von…**
I have a reservation for two in the name of…

**Wann ist das Frühstück? Ist das inklusiv?**
What time is breakfast? Is it included?

**Das Fernsehgerät in unserem Zimmer funktioniert nicht, und es gibt keine Badetücher im Badezimmer.**
The TV in our room doesn't work and there are no towels in the bathroom.

**Können Sie uns morgen früh um sieben Uhr wecken, bitte?**
Can you wake us at 7 tomorrow morning please?

**Es tut mir Leid. Ich habe meinen Schlüssel verloren.**
I'm sorry. I've lost my key.

# Holidays and Accommodation

## Camping

| | |
|---|---|
| der Abfalleimer | bin |
| das Gas | gas |
| der Platz | pitch |
| der Schlafsack | sleeping bag |
| das Spielzimmer | games room |
| die Waschmaschine | washing machine |
| der Waschraum | wash room |
| das Zelt | tent |
| zelten | to camp |

## Holiday Problems

| | |
|---|---|
| Ich habe es… liegen lassen | I have left it… |
| Ich habe… verloren | I've lost… |
| Man hat mir…. gestohlen | I've had… stolen |
| Es war… | It was… |
| | |
| die Brieftasche | the wallet |
| eine Panne haben | to break down |
| der Fahrer | driver |
| der Fotoapparat | my camera |
| das Fundbüro | lost property office |
| der Fußgänger | pedestrian |
| die Reifenpanne | flat tyre |
| der Sonnenbrand | sun burn |
| die Sonnencreme | sun cream |
| die Sorge | worry |
| der Stau | a jam, hold-up |
| die Straßenarbeiten | roadworks |
| der Straßenunfall | road accident |
| überfahren | to knock down |
| der Verkehrsunfall | road accident |
| verletzt | hurt / injured |
| die Verletzung | injury |
| die Versicherung | insurance |
| die Verspätung | delay |

## Quick Test

1 Say / write it in English:
   a) Ein Zimmer für zwei Personen im Namen Schmidt.
   b) Wir möchten drei Nächte bleiben.
   c) Wir haben keine Seife, und der Wasserhahn funktioniert nicht.

2 Say / write it in German:
   a) I would like to stay for four nights.
   b) A room with a view of the mountains.
   c) I have lost my sunglasses.

# Weather

| | | | | |
|---|---|---|---|---|
| die Aufklärung | sunny period | | der Regen | rain |
| bedeckt | overcast | | der Schatten | shade |
| das Blitzen | lightning | | schattig | shady |
| der Donner | thunder | | der Schauer | shower |
| das Eis | ice | | schlecht | bad |
| feucht | damp | | der Schnee | snow |
| das Gewitter | storm | | schön | fine |
| der Grad | degree | | die Sonne | sun |
| der Hagel | hail | | sonnig | sunny |
| heiß | hot | | der Sturm | storm |
| heiter | bright | | stürmisch | stormy |
| der Himmel | sky | | die Temperatur | temperature |
| die Hitze | heat | | trocken | dry |
| kalt | cold | | warm | warm |
| das Klima | climate | | das Wetter | weather |
| kühl | cool | | die Wettervorhersage | weather forecast |
| mild | mild | | der Wind | wind |
| nass | wet | | windig | windy |
| der Nebel | fog / mist | | die Wolken | clouds |
| nebelig | cloudy | | wolkig | cloudy |
| der Niederschlag | rain | | | |

## The Weather Forecast

**Die Wettervorhersage**
The weather forecast

**Morgen wird es im Norden bedeckt sein.**
**Höchsttemperatur 20 Grad. Im Westen Regen mit**
**Gewittern in den Bergen.**
Tomorrow it will be overcast in the north. Maximum
temperature 20 degrees. In the west, rain with storms in
the hills

**Im Osten soll es heiter sein, obwohl es am Abend**
**stürmisch werden könnte. In der Nacht kühl.**
In the east it should be bright, although in the evening it
could become stormy. Cool in the night.

**Am Wochenende wird es überall nass sein. An der**
**Küste wird es auch Nebel geben.**
At the weekend it will be wet everywhere. On the coast
there will also be fog.

## Useful Verbs

| | |
|---|---|
| **Die Sonne scheint** | The sun is shining |
| **Es friert** | It's freezing |
| **Es schneit** | It's snowing |
| **Es regnet** | It's raining |
| **Es ist schön** | It's fine / nice |
| **Es ist kalt** | It's cold |
| **Es blitzt** | It's lightning |
| **Es donnert** | It's thundering |
| **Es ist windig** | It's windy |

## Describing What the Weather Was Like

To say what the weather *was* like, you normally use the perfect tense in speaking and the imperfect tense in writing. For example:

**Es hat geschneit. / Es schneite.**
It was snowing. / It snowed.

**Es hat geregnet. / Es regnete.**
It was raining. / It rained.

**Es war furchtbar kalt.**
It was terribly cold.

**Es hat gedonnert und geblitzt. / Es donnerte und blitzte.**
It was thundering and lightning. / It thundered and there was lightning.

**Wir haben eine Woche in Griechenland verbracht, und es hat jeden Tag geregnet.**
We spent a week in Greece and it rained every day.

**Als wir in Österreich waren, war das Wetter herrlich. Wir hatten Schnee, aber es war auch sonnig.**
When we were in Austria the weather was excellent. We had snow but it was also sunny.

**In den Bergen war es kühl, aber an der Küste war es etwas milder.**
In the hills it was cool, but by the sea it was somewhat milder.

**Meine kleine Schwester hat Angst, wenn es donnert und blitzt.**
My little sister is scared when there is thunder and lightning.

## Quick Test

1. Say / write it in English:
   a) **Es donnert und es blitzt.**
   b) **Es wird später heiß sein.**
   c) **Morgen soll es sonnig sein.**
2. Say / write it in German:
   a) It is raining and it is cold.
   b) The weather forecast for Thursday is good.
   c) Today it is cloudy and overcast.

# The Environment

## My Local Environment

| | | | | | |
|---|---|---|---|---|---|
| der Bauernhof | farm | der Hügel | hill | sauber | clean |
| die Blume | flower | industriell | industrial | der Stadtrand | edge of town |
| der Bürgersteig | pavement | die Insel | island | der Stadtteil | area (of a town) |
| die Fabrik | factory | der Käfig | cage | die Umgebung | surroundings |
| das Feld | field | laut | noisy | die Umwelt | environment |
| das Feuer | fire | das Licht | light | der Verkehr | traffic |
| flach | flat | die Mitte | centre | die Wiese | meadow |
| der Fluss | river | nah | near | die Zebrastreifen | zebra crossing |
| frei | free | der Ort | place | | |
| der Frieden | peace | örtlich | local | | |
| die Gegend | area | der Rauch | smoke | | |
| die Hecke | hedge | ruhig | calm | | |

## Looking After the Environment – Useful Verbs

| | | | | | |
|---|---|---|---|---|---|
| *abschalten | to turn off / switch off | recyceln | to recycle | sich kümmern um | to worry about |
| garantieren | to guarantee | sammeln | to collect | sparen | to save |
| gebrauchen | to use | schaden | to harm | warnen | to warn |
| reinigen | to clean | schützen | to protect | * wegwerfen | to throw away |

*separable verb (see p.67)*

## Environmental Problems and Solutions

**In meiner Stadt gibt es zu viele Autos. Abgase verschmutzen die Luft.**
There are too many cars in my town. Exhaust fumes pollute the air.

**In der Stadtmitte gibt es zu viele Staus.**
In the town centre there are too many traffic jams.

**Man benutzt nicht oft genug das öffentliche Verkehrsmittel.**
People do not use public transport often enough.

**Man muss Fußgängerzonen und Fahrradwege schaffen.**
We must create pedestrian zones and cycle lanes.

**In einigen Städten sind Autos total verboten.**
In some towns cars are totally banned.

## Adjectives Used as Nouns

You can use many adjectives as nouns. Give them a capital letter, and then add the appropriate adjective ending (see p.24). For example:

- alt — old → **ein Alter** (masculine ending) — an old (man)
- arm — poor → **die Armen** (plural ending) — the poor (people)
- reisend — travelling → **die Reisenden** (plural ending) — the travellers
- klein — small → **die Kleinen** (plural ending) — the small (ones)
- metallisch — metallic → **das Metallische** (neuter ending) — the metallic (stuff)
- letzte — last → **die Letzte** (feminine ending) — the last (woman)

## Other Ways to Form Nouns

In your exam you may come across nouns that look unfamiliar, but there are a few simple rules that may help you to work out what they mean.

Nouns may be formed by taking a verb, removing the -en and adding -ung. For example:

- **übernacht**en ➡ eine **Übernacht**ung
  to spend the night   an overnight stay
- **überrasch**en ➡ eine **Überrasch**ung
  to surprise   a surprise
- **wandern** ➡ eine **Wander**ung
  to go on a hike   a hike

The ending -heit or -keit may be added to an adjective to create another noun. For example:

- **schön** ➡ die **Schön**heit
  beautiful   beauty
- **glücklich** ➡ die **Glücklich**keit
  happy   happiness

The ending -schaft may be added to a noun to create another noun. For example:

- **Freund** ➡ die **Freund**schaft
  friend   friendship

It will also help if you remember that German speakers often join two or more nouns together to make a longer noun.

The gender of the 'compound noun' is taken from the last noun in the compound, e.g. **Das Lehrerzimmer** is neuter because **das Zimmer** is neuter.

### Quick Test

1. Say / write it in English:
   a) **In der Stadtmitte gibt es zu viel Verkehr.**
   b) **Wir sollen uns um die Umwelt kümmern.**
   c) **Diese Gegend ist ruhig und sauber.**
2. Say / write it in German:
   a) We recycle glass and paper.
   b) We must protect the environment.
   c) My town is not very clean.

Cover up the English in the following list and try to work out what the German words mean:

|  |  |
|---|---|
| die Arbeitszeit | work time |
| der Badeanzug | bathing suit |
| der Busbahnhof | bus station |
| der Computerprogrammierer | computer programmer |
| die Computerspiele | computer games |
| die Einkaufstasche | shopping bag |
| das Familienmitglied | family member |
| das Familienzimmer | family room |
| das Fitnesszentrum | fitness centre |
| die Hausnummer | house number |
| die Klassenfahrt | class trip |
| das Klassenzimmer | classroom |
| der Kleiderschrank | wardrobe |
| die Kunstgalerie | art gallery |
| das Lehrerzimmer | staff room |
| die Magenschmerzen | stomach ache |
| das Mineralwasser | mineral water |
| die Mittagspause | lunch break |
| die Öffnungszeiten | opening times |
| die Rassenprobleme | race issues |
| der Regenmantel | raincoat |
| der Schreibtisch | desk |
| das Schreibwarengeschäft | stationery shop |
| die Schülerzeitung | school newspaper |
| das Schwimmbad | swimming pool |
| die Sommerferien | summer holidays |
| die Sonnenbrille | sun glasses |
| das Sportzentrum | sports centre |
| das Sprachlabor | language lab |
| die Straßenbahnhaltestelle | tram stop |
| die Straßenkarte | street map |
| das Tabakwarengeschäft | tobacconist shop |
| der Tellerwäscher | person who washes dishes |
| das Toilettenpapier | toilet paper |
| die Touristeninformation | tourist information centre |
| das Trinkwasser | drinking water |
| die Umweltprobleme | environmental problems |
| das Wartezimmer | waiting room |
| die Waschmaschine | washing machine |
| der Weihnachtsmarkt | Christmas market |
| das Zweibettzimmer | twin room |

# Global Issues

Here are some words that are useful for talking about issues affecting the world:

| | |
|---|---|
| **biologisch** | biological |
| **bleifrei** | unleaded |
| **das Altpapier** | used paper |
| **das Benzin** | petrol |
| **das Eisen** | iron |
| **das Erdbeben** | earthquake |
| **das Experiment** | experiment |
| **das Jahrhundert** | century |
| **das Kohlengas** | carbon gas |
| **der Kunststoff** | synthetic material |
| **das Loch** | hole |
| **das Metall** | metal |
| **die Natur** | nature |
| **das Öl** | oil |
| **das Opfer** | victim |
| **das Pestizid** | pesticide |
| **der Sauerstoff** | oxygen |
| **das Treibhausgas** | greenhouse gas |
| **der Abfall** | rubbish / waste |
| **der Biomüll** | organic waste |
| **der Krieg** | war |
| **der Mond** | moon |
| **der Öltanker** | oil tanker |
| **der Strom** | electricity |
| **der Treibhauseffekt** | the greenhouse effect |
| **die Abgase** | waste gases |
| **die Elektrizität** | electricity |
| **die Erde** | Earth |

| | |
|---|---|
| **die Gegenwart** | presence |
| **die Kernkraft** | nuclear energy |
| **die Kohle** | coal |
| **die Luft** | air |
| **die Mülltonne** | waste skip, dust bin |
| **die Pappe** | cardboard |
| **die Pflanze** | plant |
| **Plastik** | plastic |
| **die Ruhe** | calm |
| **die Sonnenkraft** | solar power |
| **die Spraydose** | aerosol |
| **die Verschmutzung** | pollution |
| **die Welle** | wave |
| **die Welt** | the world |
| **die Windkraft** | wind power |
| **kaputt** | broken |
| **kürzlich** | recent |
| **organisch** | organic |
| **sauber** | clean |
| **saurer Regen** | acid rain |
| **schmutzig** | dirty |
| **ultraviolette Strahlen** | ultraviolet rays |
| **umweltfeindlich** | environmentally harmful |
| **umweltfreundlich** | environmentally friendly |
| **verschmutzt** | polluted |
| **weltweit** | worldwide |
| **die Ozonschicht** | ozone layer |
| **zerbrechlich** | fragile |

## Useful Verbs

| | | | | | |
|---|---|---|---|---|---|
| **abschaffen** | to abolish | **produzieren** | to produce | **sparen** | to save |
| **bauen** | to build | **reduzieren** | to reduce | **verbessern** | to improve |
| **beschädigen** | to damage | **sauber machen** | to clean | **verschwinden** | to disappear |
| **besorgen** | to provide | **schöpfen** | to create | **wachsen** | to increase / grow |
| **drohen** | to threaten | **schützen** | to protect | **zerstören** | to destroy |

## Animals

| | | | | |
|---|---|---|---|---|
| **der Affe** | monkey | **das Huhn** | hen | |
| **der Bär** | bear | **das Insekt** | insect | |
| **die Biene** | bee | **das Schaf** | sheep | |
| **der Elefant** | elephant | **das Schwein** | pig | |
| **der Fisch** | fish | **der Tiger** | tiger | |
| **die Fliege** | fly | **der Walfisch** | whale | |
| **der Fuchs** | fox | **die Wespe** | wasp | |

## Sharing Your Concerns

| | |
|---|---|
| **der Krieg** | war |
| **das Verbrechen** | crime |
| **der Terrorismus** | terrorism |
| **die Armut** | poverty |
| **die Hungersnot** | famine |

**Saurer Regen ist ein großes Problem für die Umwelt.**
Acid rain is a big problem for the environment.

**Ich bin überzeugt, dass wir das Problem des Treibhauseffekts lösen müssen.**
I am convinced that we must solve the problem of the greenhouse effect.

**Windkraft, Wellenkraft und Sonnenkraft – das ist die Energie der Zukunft.**
Wind power, wave power and solar power – that is the energy of the future.

**Es ist wichtig, dass wir zusammenkommen, um diese Themen zu besprechen.**
It is important that we come together to discuss these issues.

### Quick Test

1. Say / write it in English:
   a) **Der Treibhauseffekt ist ein großes Problem für uns alle.**
   b) **Wir müssen die Tiere schützen.**
   c) **Wir benutzen zuviel Kohlengas.**
2. Say / write it in German:
   a) I am concerned about pollution.
   b) We use too many aerosols.
   c) The ultraviolet rays are dangerous.

# Life in Other Countries

## Food in Other Countries

| | |
|---|---|
| Man isst es mit… | It's eaten with… |
| Man macht es aus… | It's made out of… |
| | |
| das Ausland | abroad |
| das Essen | food |
| das Gericht | dish |
| die Gewohnheit | habit |
| gewürzt | spicy |
| das Kochen | cooking |
| die Marmelade | jam |
| mild | mild |
| die Schale | bowl |
| die Spezialität | speciality |
| süß | sweet |
| die Zutaten | ingredients |

**Dieses Gericht ist eine Spezialität von Nordafrika. Es ist lecker!**
This dish is a speciality of North Africa. It is delicious!

**Sie kochen oft draußen, weil es so heiß ist.**
They often cook outdoors because it is so hot.

**Man macht es aus Fleisch (oft Lamm), Gemüse, Zwiebeln und Tomaten.**
It's made with meat (often lamb), vegetables, onions and tomatoes.

**Sie essen diesen Kuchen zu Weihnachten. Die Zutaten sind Obst und Marzipan.**
They eat this cake at Christmas. The ingredients are fruit and marzipan.

## Daily life in Other Countries

| | |
|---|---|
| der Ausländer | foreigner |
| ausländisch | foreign |
| einverstanden | agreed |
| entfernt | distant |
| ernst | serious |
| das Tier | animal |
| der Tourismus | tourism |
| der Unterschied | difference |
| der Wohnort | place where you live |
| die Erfahrung | experience |
| falsch | wrong |
| faszinierend | fascinating |
| vorherrschend | predominant |
| ideal | ideal |
| multikulturell | multicultural |
| normal | normal |
| Schlange stehen | to form a queue |
| das Souvenir | souvenir |
| das Spielzeug | toy |
| staatlich | state |
| typisch | typical |
| überall | everywhere |
| überhaupt nicht | not at all |

**Tourismus it sehr wichtig für dieses Land.**
Tourism is very important for this country.

**Es gibt viele wichtige Unterschiede zwischen diesem Land und Großbritannien.**
There are many important differences between this country and Britain.

**Ich finde die multikulturelle Gesellschaft faszinierend.**
I think the multicultural society is fascinating.

**Die traditionelle Kleidung ist sehr bunt.**
The traditional clothing is very colourful.

## Useful Verbs

| *<u>aus</u>kommen | to get along with |
|---|---|
| erklären | to explain |
| erlauben | to allow |
| erzählen | to tell |
| wohnen | to live |

*separable verb (see p.67)

## Word Order in Complex Sentences

You already know that in *subordinate clauses* you have to send the verb to the end of the sentence (see p.37).

If the sentence continues *after* the end of the subordinate clause, add a comma and make the main verb the next word after the comma.

*Think: 'verb – comma – verb'*

Examples:
- **Weil das Wetter kalt ist, bleibe ich zu Hause.**
  Because the weather is cold, I stay at home.
- **Wenn ich nach Italien fahre, esse ich immer gern eine Pizza.**
  When I go to Italy I always like to eat a pizza.
- **Weil es sehr heiß ist, schlafen sie am Nachmittag.**
  Because it is very hot they sleep in the afternoon.

Note how you can use the imperfect subjunctive (see p.37) in structures like the following:
- **Wenn wir mehr Geld hätten, wäre es möglich, diese Probleme zu lösen.**
  If we had more money it would be possible to solve these problems.

## Quick Test

**1** Say / write it in English:
  a) **Man isst dieses Gericht am Abend.**
  b) **Ich finde die Unterschiede faszinierend.**
  c) **Wenn man in Großbritannien ist, muss man normalerweise Schlange stehen.**
  d) **Die Spezialität der Region ist sehr süß.**

**2** Say / write it in German:
  a) It's made of fish. It is spicy.
  b) It's eaten with bread.
  c) This dish is very mild.

# Practice Questions

## Reading

**1** Read the sentences below and match them to the statements that follow.

    **A**   Meiner Meinung nach recycelt man nicht genug Glas. Das ist ein großes Problem.

    **B**   Ich sammle Altpapier. Das ist gut für die Umwelt.

    **C**   Zu Hause, wenn es kalt ist, ziehe ich eine Wolljacke an, statt die Heizung anzumachen.

    **D**   Ich bade mich nie; ich dusche mich immer. Das ist umweltfreundlicher.

    **E**   Wenn ich ein Zimmer verlasse, mache ich immer das Licht aus.

    **F**   Wenn man Lebensmittel einpackt, benutzt man zuviel Pappe und Plastik.

**a)** Saving electricity _____

**b)** Saving water _____

**c)** Recycling paper _____

**d)** Packaging _____

**e)** Avoiding over-heating the house _____

**f)** Recycling glass _____

**2** Read the passage and then answer, in English, the questions that follow.

> **Sabrina spricht über ihre Ferien.**
>
> **Vor zwei Jahren bin ich in die Schweiz gefahren, um einen Skiurlaub zu machen. Ich bin im Februar gefahren. Ich bin zehn Tage geblieben. Ich bin mit dem Reisebus gefahren. Die Reise war ziemlich lang und ermüdend. Wir sind in einer Ferienwohnung geblieben. Jeden Tag habe bin ich Ski gelaufen. Ich habe auch ein paar lange Wanderungen in den Bergen gemacht. Die Landschaft war toll, aber es war furchtbar kalt! Es hat viel geschneit. Am Abend haben wir Schach gespielt.**

**a)** Where did Sabrina go for her holiday? _____

**b)** Why did she go there? _____

**c)** How long did she stay? _____

**d)** How did she get there? _____

**e)** What did she think about her journey? _____

**f)** What sort of accommodation did she stay in? _____

**g)** What was the weather like? _____

**h)** What did she do in the evenings? _____

## Speaking

**3** Give a full response, in German, to each of the questions below. Say your answer out loud.

**a)** Wo verbringst du gern deine Ferien?

**b)** Wohin bist du letztes Jahr gefahren?

**c)** Was hast du im Urlaub gemacht?

**d)** Wie war das Wetter?

**e)** Was machst du, um die Umwelt zu schützen?

## Writing

**4** You're writing about a holiday you've been on. Write about each of the following, in German.

**a)** Where you went and how you got there.

**b)** What you did whilst on holiday.

**c)** Where you'd like to go next year and why.

**5** You're writing about your plans to make your town more environmentally friendly. Write about each of the following, in German.

**a)** What you think the main problems are with your local environment.

**b)** What you would do to reduce these problems.

**c)** Why it is important to care about what happens to the environment.

# Strong and Irregular Verbs

## Table of Common Strong and Irregular Verbs

The following table is not a complete list. Grammar reference books and dictionaries will provide a full list.

Separable verbs are not listed, for example, **fangen** is shown, but **anfangen** is not.

*\* indicates auxiliary verb **sein** in the perfect / pluperfect tense.*

| Infinitive | Irregular Present (er / sie / es) | Imperfect (er / sie / es) | Past Participle | Meaning |
|---|---|---|---|---|
| beginnen | – | begann | begonnen | to begin |
| biegen | – | bog | gebogen | to bend |
| bieten | – | bot | geboten | to offer |
| bitten | – | bat | gebeten | to ask |
| bleiben | – | blieb | geblieben* | to stay |
| brechen | bricht | brach | gebrochen | to break |
| bringen | – | brachte | gebracht | to bring |
| denken | – | dachte | gedacht | to think |
| dürfen | darf | durfte | gedurft | to be allowed to |
| empfehlen | empfiehlt | empfahl | empfohlen | to recommend |
| essen | isst | aß | gegessen | to eat |
| fahren | fährt | fuhr | gefahren* | to go, drive |
| fallen | fällt | fiel | gefallen* | to fall |
| fangen | fängt | fing | gefangen | to catch |
| finden | – | fand | gefunden | to find |
| fliegen | – | flog | geflogen* | to fly |
| geben | gibt | gab | gegeben | to give |
| gehen | – | ging | gegangen* | to go, walk |
| gelingen | – | gelang | gelungen* | to succeed |
| genießen | – | genoss | genossen | to enjoy |
| geschehen | geschieht | geschah | geschehen* | to happen |
| gewinnen | – | gewann | gewonnen | to win |
| greifen | – | griff | gegriffen | to grab, grasp |
| haben | hat | hatte | gehabt | to have |
| halten | hält | hielt | gehalten | to stop |
| heißen | – | hieß | geheißen | to be called |
| helfen | hilft | half | geholfen | to help |
| kennen | – | kannte | gekannt | to know (people) |
| kommen | – | kam | gekommen* | to come |
| können | kann | konnte | gekonnt | to be able to |
| lassen | lässt | ließ | gelassen | to leave |
| laufen | läuft | lief | gelaufen* | to run |
| leiden | – | litt | gelitten | to suffer |
| leihen | – | lieh | geliehen | to lend |

# Strong and Irregular Verbs

| Infinitive | Irregular Present (er / sie / es) | Imperfect (er / sie / es) | Past Participle | Meaning |
|---|---|---|---|---|
| lesen | liest | las | gelesen | to read |
| liegen | – | lag | gelegen | to lie (on beach, etc) |
| lügen | – | log | gelogen | to tell a lie |
| mögen | mag | mochte | gemocht | to like |
| müssen | muss | musste | gemusst | to have to |
| nehmen | nimmt | nahm | genommen | to take |
| nennen | – | nannte | genannt | to name |
| raten | rät | riet | geraten | to guess / to advise |
| reiten | – | ritt | geritten* | to ride (horses) |
| rufen | – | rief | gerufen | to call |
| scheinen | – | schien | geschienen, gescheint | to shine |
| schlafen | schläft | schlief | geschlafen | to sleep |
| schlagen | schlägt | schlug | geschlagen | to hit |
| schließen | – | schloss | geschlossen | to shut |
| schneiden | – | schnitt | geschnitten | to cut |
| schreiben | – | schrieb | geschrieben | to write |
| sehen | sieht | sah | gesehen | to see |
| sein | ist | war | gewesen* | to be |
| sitzen | – | saß | gesessen | to sit |
| sollen | soll | sollte | gesollt | to be supposed to |
| sprechen | spricht | sprach | gesprochen | to speak |
| stehen | – | stand | gestanden | to stand |
| stehlen | stiehlt | stahl | gestohlen | to steal |
| steigen | – | stieg | gestiegen* | to climb |
| sterben | stirbt | starb | gestorben* | to die |
| tragen | trägt | trug | getragen | to wear, carry |
| treffen | trifft | traf | getroffen | to meet |
| treiben | – | trieb | getrieben | to do (sport) |
| trinken | – | trank | getrunken | to drink |
| tun | – | tat | getan | to do |
| vergessen | vergisst | vergaß | vergessen | to forget |
| verlieren | – | verlor | verloren | to lose |
| verschwinden | – | verschwand | verschwunden* | to disappear |
| waschen | wäscht | wusch | gewaschen | to wash |
| werden | wird | wurde | geworden* | to become |
| werfen | wirft | warf | geworfen | to throw |
| wissen | weiß | wusste | gewusst | to know (facts) |
| ziehen | – | zog | gezogen | to pull |

# Word Bank

## Masculine Nouns

| | | | | | |
|---|---|---|---|---|---|
| der Abschluss | end / conclusion | der Kandidat | candidate | der Punkt | point |
| der Anspitzer | pencil sharpener | der Krankenwagen | ambulance | der Scheck | cheque |
| der Ausflug | trip | der Lohn | wage | der Schmerz | pain |
| der Beamte(r) | official | der Maler | painter | der Typ | guy / bloke |
| der Brennstoff | fuel | der Meter | metre | der Vormittag | morning |
| der Briefkasten | letter box | der Moment | moment | der Vorname | forename |
| der Briefumschlag | envelope | der Nachmittag | afternoon | der Vorteil | advantage |
| der Buchstabe | letter | der Plan | plan | der Waschsalon | laundry / laundrette |
| der Geburtsort | place of birth | der Postbote | postman | der Zentimeter | centimetre |
| der Heimleiter | warden | der Priester | priest | der Zuschauer | spectator |
| der Helm | helmet | der Projektor | projector | | |

## Feminine Nouns

| | | | | | |
|---|---|---|---|---|---|
| die AG | Co. / company | die Hilfe | help | die Schere | scissors |
| die Briefmarke | stamp | die Leiter | ladder | die Therapie | therapy |
| die Beamte | official | die Menge | crowd | die Umkleidekabine | changing room |
| die Couch | couch | die Messe | exhibition | die Versammlung | gathering / assembly |
| die Dame | lady | die Million | a million | die Vorliebe | preference |
| die Ehrlichkeit | honesty | die Ordnung | order / tidiness | die Wäscherei | laundry |
| die Gruppe | group | die Polizei | police | die Wohltätigkeit | charity |
| die Halle | hall | die Postkarte | postcard | die Zahl | number |
| die Heimleitung | management of hostel | die Postleitzahl | post code | die Zahnbürste | toothbrush |
| | | | | die Zahnpasta | toothpaste |

## Neuter Nouns

| | | | | | |
|---|---|---|---|---|---|
| das Alter | age | das Ende | end | das Paket | parcel |
| das Arbeitszimmer | work room | das Gegenteil | opposite | das Quadrat | square |
| das Betttuch | sheet | das Holz | wood | das Rechteck | right angle |
| das Bewusstsein | consciousness | das Image | image | das Schaufenster | shop window |
| das Datum | date | das Kunstwerk | art work | das Tierheim | shelter |
| das Detail | detail | das Lokal | pub | das Verfallsdatum | use by date |
| das Dreieck | triangle | das Maß | mass | das Wort | word |
| | | | | das Zeichnen | drawing |

## Plural Nouns

| | |
|---|---|
| die Eltern | parents |
| die FCKWs | CFCs |
| die Hausschuhe | slippers |

## Verbs

| | | | | | |
|---|---|---|---|---|---|
| akzeptieren | to accept | beschließen | to decide | entwerten | to devalue |
| *(an)bauen | to build | besichtigen | to view | erfüllen | to fulfill |
| Angst haben | to be afraid | besitzen | to possess | fallen | to fall |
| *(an)klopfen | to knock | betreten | to enter | folgen | to follow |
| *anspucken | to spit at | brechen | to break | führen | to lead |
| antworten | to answer | danken | to thank | halten | to stop |
| auf sein | to be up (not in bed) | dauern | to last | *hereinkommen | to come in |
| *ausführen | to export / carry out | denken | to think | klingeln | to ring / tinkle |
| *ausrichten | to equip | *einstellen | to put in / take on | klopfen | to knock |
| *aussetzen | to stop / interrupt | enden | to end | kritisieren | to criticise |
| beleidigen | to offend | entsorgen | to dispose of | leiden | to stand / bear / suffer |

*separable verb (see p.67)

## Verbs (cont.)

| | | | | | |
|---|---|---|---|---|---|
| machen | to do / make | schließen | to close / shut | vergeben | to award / allocate |
| *nachgehen | to go after | sehen | to see | verpacken | to pack |
| nennen | to name | sich schämen | to be ashamed | verpassen | to miss (a bus, etc.) |
| nerven | to annoy | sich scheiden lassen | to get divorced | *vorgehen | to happen / proceed |
| öffnen | to open | sich setzen | to sit down | *vorziehen | to prefer |
| Recht haben | to be right | sich trennen | to separate | *weiterfahren | to travel on |
| rennen | to race | sich *vorstellen | to introduce oneself | wissen | to know |
| schenken | to give (as a present) | treten | to tread / kick | zahlen | to pay |
| schießen | to shoot | überwachen | to watch over | zeigen | to show |
| schlagen | to beat | Unrecht haben | to be wrong | *zustimmen | to agree |

*separable verb

## Adjectives / Adverbs

| | | | | | |
|---|---|---|---|---|---|
| enorm | enormous | eng | narrow | privat | private |
| ähnlich | similar | fertig | ready / finished | richtig | right |
| ängstlich | fearful | fest | firm | scharf | sharp |
| anonym | anonymous | gebrochen | broken | selbständig | independent |
| beide | both | heftig | hefty | sensibel | sensitive |
| berühmt | famous | informativ | informative | überrascht | surprised |
| besetzt | occupied | leer | empty | unordentlich | untidy |
| bestimmt | certain | lehrreich | informative | verschieden | various |
| breit | broad | leicht | easy | viereckig | rectangular |
| dreieckig | triangular | mittelgroß | medium sized | voll | full |
| dünn | thin | offen | open | weich | soft |
| ehemalig | former | ordentlich | orderly / tidy | wichtig | important |
| ehrlich | honest | plötzlich | sudden | wirklich | really |
| | | | | witzig | funny / joking |

## Other Useful Words

| | | | | | |
|---|---|---|---|---|---|
| abgesehen davon | apart from | ganz | completely | so viel / viele… wie | as much / many… as |
| all | all | gestern | yesterday | so… wie | as… as |
| angenommen | adopted | (hier)her | this way / here | trotzdem | nevertheless |
| außen | outside | (hier)hin | that way / away | übermorgen | day after tomorrow |
| außerdem | besides | heraus / hinaus | out | umgeben von | surrounded by |
| beiliegend | enclosed | herein / hinein | in | viele | many |
| besonders | especially | irgend | some / any | vor kurzem | recently |
| damals | then | mindestens | at least | vorbei | past |
| denn | because | montags (etc.) | every Monday (etc.) | vorgestern | day before yesterday |
| dennoch | yet | nach oben | upstairs | vorher | beforehand |
| der / die / das gleiche | the same | nach unten | downstairs | wenigstens | at least |
| deshalb | therefore | nachts | at night | wieder | again |
| deswegen | for this reason | nirgends | nowhere | woher? | where from? |
| drittens | thirdly | nun | now | zu Ende | at an end / finished |
| einzeln | individual(ly); separate(ly) | nur | only | zweitens | secondly |
| etwa | approximately | ohne Zweifel | without doubt | zwo = zwei | two (on telephone) |
| fast | almost | selbst | even / oneself | | |

# Answers

## The Essentials

**Quick Test – Page 9**
1. **a)** Today is the 24th of June.
   **b)** It is now 5.15 (pm).

2. **a)** Ich heiße Jonathan. Man schreibt es J-O-N-A-T-H-A-N.
   **b)** Entschuldigung. Wo ist der Bahnhof?

## Home Life and Personal Information

**Quick Test – Page 11**
1. **a)** My father is thirty-nine.
   **b)** My mother is called Laura.
   **c)** My sister has a rabbit.
   **d)** I have two brothers, but no sisters.
2. **a)** Mein Vater ist fünfundvierzig Jahre alt.
   **b)** Meine Mutter hat einen Bruder.
   **c)** Ich bin Einzelkind.
   **d)** Meine Schwester hat ein Pferd.

**Page 13**
1. **a)** My father has short hair.
   **b)** My mother is very slim.
   **c)** My sister has brown eyes.
2. **a)** Mein Bruder hat lange Haare.
   **b)** Ich habe schwarze Haare und braune Augen.
   **c)** Wie alt ist deine Schwester?

**Page 15**
1. **a)** My friend is always good fun.
   **b)** My brother is selfish and mean.
2. **a)** Mein Vater ist freundlich und immer optimistisch.
   **b)** Meine Schwester ist manchmal eifersüchtig.

**Page 17**
1. **a)** My sister is smaller than me.
   **b)** My best friend is more intelligent than me.
   **c)** Her granddad is widowed.
2. **a)** Mein bester Freund / Meine beste Freundin ist ein bisschen verrückt.
   **b)** Mein Bruder ist nie höflich.
   **c)** Mein Onkel ist immer lustig.

**Page 19**
1. **a)** I would like to find the ideal partner.
   **b)** I hope to have three children.
   **c)** I will work in America.
2. **a)** Ich hoffe, reich zu werden.
   **b)** Ich möchte in Amerika studieren.
   **c)** Ich möchte glücklich sein.

**Page 21**
1. **a)** I want to complain about unemployment.
   **b)** There is too much homelessness here. I find that unjust.
   **c)** One should combat racism.
2. **a)** Man will gegen die Hungersnot kämpfen.
   **b)** Ein Problem ist die Diskriminierung.
   **c)** Wir sollten ihre Rechte schützen.

**Page 23**
1. **a)** My bedroom is on the first floor.
   **b)** I regularly set the table and I often cook.
   **c)** The toilet is downstairs.
2. **a)** Der Garten ist ziemlich groß.
   **b)** Meine Hausnummer ist vierzehn.
   **c)** Ich koche oft aber ich bügele nie.

**Page 25**
1. **a)** Our flat is in a large block of flats.
   **b)** My house is on the edge of town not far from the sea.
   **c)** We always eat in the dining room.
2. **a)** Ich arbeite in meinem Schlafzimmer.
   **b)** Meine Schwester kommt um fünf Uhr (siebzehn Uhr) nach Hause.
   **c)** Wir sitzen im Wohnzimmer und sehen fern.

**Page 27**
1. **a)** Our town is in the north.
   **b)** It is a big industrial town.
   **c)** In the town centre there is a pedestrian precinct.
2. **a)** Unsere Stadt liegt im Süden.
   **b)** Man kann den Zoo oder die Kunstgalerie besuchen.
   **c)** Ich mag das Einkaufszentrum und das Hallenbad.

**Page 29**
1. **a)** Go straight on as far as the traffic lights, then turn left.
   **b)** Where is the station please?
   **c)** When does the next train for Ostende leave?
2. **a)** Wie komme ich zur U-bahnstation bitte?
   **b)** Gibt es hier ein Wartezimmer?
   **c)** Wann kommt der Zug an?

**Practice Questions – Pages 30-31**
1. **a)** sportlich **b)** sparsam **c)** launisch **d)** faul **e)** fleißig **f)** ungeduldig
2. **a)** North Germany, near Bremen.
   **b)** Go on hikes, go shopping, do sport.
   **c)** Yes, because there is a lot to do and see.
   **d)** He wouldn't like to live there. It is too quiet and there is nothing to do.
   **e)** In England (in a large flat) because he likes speaking English.

**3. Example answers:**
**a)** Mein Geburtstag ist der dritte Mai. *My birthday is the third of May.* **b)** Ich bin mittelgroß. Ich habe blaue Augen und braune Haare. *I am medium sized. I have blue eyes and brown hair.*
**c)** Ich bin ziemlich faul aber ich bin freundlich und immer gut gelaunt. *I am quite lazy but I am friendly and I am always in a good mood.* **d)** Ich habe eine Schwester und einen Bruder. *I have one sister and one brother.*
**e)** Mein Haus ist ziemlich klein. Es ist ein Reihenhaus. Wir haben drei Schlafzimmer und einen kleinen Garten. *My house is quite small. It is a terraced house. We have three bedrooms and a small garden.* **f)** Ich wohne am Stadtrand. Hier sind viele Geschäfte, auch ein Park und ein Sportzentrum. *I live on the edge of town. There are lots of shops here, also a park and a sports centre.* **g)** Ich würde lieber in der Stadt wohnen. Hier sind viele Geschäfte, man kann ins Kino oder ins Sportzentrum gehen. Meine Freunde und Freundinnen wohnen auch hier. *I would rather live in the town. There are lots of shops here and you can go to the cinema or to the sports centre. My friends (male and female) also live here.*

**4. Example answers:**
**a)** Sie ist etwa fünfzehn Jahre alt. Sie hat kurze, lockige Haare, braune oder grüne Augen, und sie ist mittelgroß. Sie ist launisch und ein bisschen egoistisch. *She is about fifteen years old. She has short curly hair, brown or green eyes and she is medium sized. She is moody and a bit selfish.*
**b)** Sie versteht sich gut mit ihren Schwestern, aber sie hat auch einen jüngeren Bruder, und sie streiten sich immer. *She gets on well with her sisters, but she also has a younger brother and they argue all the time.*
**c)** Sie singt sehr laut, wenn sie allein ist, und sie trägt gern eine große, rote Sonnenbrille. *She sings very loudly when she is alone, and she likes to wear big red sunglasses.*

**5. Example answers:**
**a)** Wenn ich die Schule verlasse, hoffe ich, auf die Universität zu gehen. Ich will Medizin studieren, weil ich Arzt / Ärztin werden will. *When I leave school I hope to go to university. I want to study medicine because I want to become a doctor.* **b)** Ich möchte im Ausland wohnen, vielleicht in Afrika oder Asien, wo ich als Arzt / Ärztin arbeiten kann. *I would like to live abroad, perhaps in Africa or Asia, where I can work as a doctor.*
**c)** Ich habe Frankreich schon besucht, aber ich möchte auch nach Amerika oder Kanada reisen. Diese Länder sind sehr interessant für mich. *I have already visited France but I would like to travel to America or Canada. These countries are very interesting for me.*

## School and Work

**Quick Test – Page 33**
1. **a)** My favourite subject is English. I always get good marks.
   **b)** Geography is boring. The teacher is too old.
   **c)** The lessons begin at half past eight.
2. **a)** Ich lerne gern Deutsch. Es ist sehr interessant.
   **b)** Ich mag nicht Mathe. Das ist zu schwer. Das ist Blödsinn!
   **c)** Das Essen in der Kantine ist sehr gut.

**Page 35**
1. **a)** The boys wear a black jacket and the girls wear a blue skirt.
   **b)** We always have to do our homework.
   **c)** We must always arrive punctually in the mornings.
2. **a)** Wir dürfen keine Ohrringe tragen.
   **b)** Die Uniform ist schick aber ein bisschen altmodisch.
   **c)** Die Jungen in meiner Klasse sind immer unhöflich.

**Page 37**
1. **a)** Peter has to do a detention because he got bad marks.
   **b)** Laura makes a lot of mistakes because she can't add up well.
   **c)** We have too much stress in school!
2. **a)** Es gibt kein Bullying in meiner Schule, und die Disziplin ist gut.
   **b)** Die Lehrer arbeiten fleißig. Sie korrigieren jede Woche unsere Arbeit.
   **c)** Meine Durchschnittsnote war ausgezeichnet!

**Page 39**
1. **a)** I want to become a nurse.
   **b)** My friend wants to go to university.
   **c)** At the end of the year I hope to start an apprenticeship.
2. **a)** Nächstes Jahr will ich als Mechaniker arbeiten.
   **b)** Nach zwei Jahren will ich die Schule verlassen.
   **c)** Wenn ich einundzwanzig bin, will ich im Ausland arbeiten.

**Page 41**
1. **a)** I do part-time work in a café.
   **b)** I earn six pounds per hour.
   **c)** With my pocket money I buy school things and magazines.
   **d)** How can I best find a second job?
2. **a)** Mit meinem Taschengeld kaufe ich Geschenke und Computerspiele.
   **b)** Ich will Geld sparen, um Schmuck zu kaufen.
   **c)** Ich sorge für meinen jungen Bruder.
   **d)** Mein(e) Freund(in) arbeitet von zu Hause.

**Page 43**
1. **a)** I worked in an office for two weeks.
   **b)** I didn't earn any money but the experience was fun.
   **c)** He hated his work experience. It was a waste of time.
2. **a)** Ich habe Briefe geschrieben und am Computer gearbeitet.
   **b)** Ich habe um halb sechs (fünf Uhr dreißig) Feierabend gehabt.
   **c)** Ich bin jeden Tag mit dem Bus gefahren.

**Practice Questions – Pages 44-45**
1. **a)** Sabine and Amira **b)** Dieter **c)** Erkan **d)** Sabine **e)** Erkan **f)** Sabine **g)** Dieter **h)** She says the teachers have no time for the students and don't get on well with them (they are impolite).

**2. Example answers:**
**a)** Meine Schule ist eine große Gesamtschule. Hier sind mehr als neunhundert Schüler und Schülerinnen. *My school is a large comprehensive. There are more than nine hundred pupils here.* **b)** Wir kommen um acht Uhr fünfzehn in die Schule. Die erste Stunde beginnt um acht Uhr zwanzig. Die Mittagspause ist um zwölf Uhr fünfzehn. Das dauert fünfzig Minuten. Am Nachmittag haben wir zwei Stunden, und wir gehen um drei Uhr nach Hause. *We come to school at 8.15. The first lesson begins at 8.20. The lunch break is at 12.15. It lasts for 50 minutes. In the afternoon we have two lessons and we go home at 3 o'clock.* **c)** Die Jungen tragen ein weißes Hemd, eine schwarze Hose und eine dunkelblaue Jacke. Die Mädchen tragen ein weißes Hemd und einen blauen Rock. Alle Schüler und Schülerinnen tragen eine schwarz-rote, gestreifte Krawatte. *The boys wear a white shirt, black trousers and a dark blue jacket. The girls wear a white shirt and a blue skirt. All pupils wear a black and red striped tie.* **d)** Mein Lieblingsfach ist natürlich Deutsch! *My favourite subject is German of course!* **e)** Es ist sehr interessant, der Lehrer/die Lehrerin ist sehr gut, und ich bekomme immer gute Noten. *It is very interesting, the teacher is very good and I always get good marks.* **f)** Ich mag Sport nicht. *I do not like sport.* **g)** Ich bin gar nicht sportlich, und der Lehrer/die Lehrerin ist immer schlechter Laune. *I am not at all sporty, and the teacher is always in a bad mood.* **h)** Ich hoffe, auf die Universität zu gehen. Ich will Physik und Chemie studieren. *I hope to go to university. I want to study physics and chemistry.* **i)** Ich finde Wissenschaften sehr interessant. Physik ist mein Lieblingsfach. *I think sciences are very interesting. Physics is my favourite subject.* **j)** Ich will Ingenieur werden. *I want to become an engineer.*

**3. Example answers:**
**a)** Die Schule ist ziemlich altmodisch. Wir haben viele alte Klassenzimmer aber keine Turnhalle, und die Kantine ist zu klein. *The school is rather old fashioned. We have lots of old classrooms but no gymnasium, and the canteen is too small.* **b)** Meiner Meinung nach sollten alle Schüler und Schülerinnen drei Fremdsprachen lernen, zum Beispiel Chinesisch oder Japanisch. Sprachen sind sehr wichtig in der modernen Welt. *In my opinion all the students ought to study three foreign languages, for example Chinese or Japanese. Languages are very important in the modern world.* **c)** Es ist gut, dass sowohl die reichen als auch die armen Schüler und Schülerinnen die gleichen Kleider tragen. Man braucht sich nicht um die Mode zu kümmern. *It is good that both the rich as well as the poor students wear the same clothes. They don't need to bother about fashion.*

**4. Example answers:**
**a)** Ich interessiere mich sehr für Computer. Wenn ich den ganzen Tag am Computer sitze, dann bin ich glücklich. Das ist mein idealer Job. *I am interested very much in computers. If I sit at a computer for the entire day then I am happy. That is my ideal job.* **b)** Ich mag Mathe und Computerwissenschaft. Mit guten Noten in diesen Fächern wird es nicht schwer sein, eine Stelle zu finden. *I love maths and computer studies. With good marks in these subjects it will not be difficult to find a job.* **c)** Ich möchte in Manchester wohnen und arbeiten, weil meine Familie und meine Freunde auch hier wohnen. *I would like to live and work in Manchester because my family and my friends also live here.*

## Lifestyle

**Quick Test – Page 47**
1. **a)** My stomach hurts.
   **b)** I feel dizzy all the time.
   **c)** My back hurts.
   **d)** I'd like to make an appointment. When is the surgery open?
2. **a)** Mir tut der Zahn weh.
   **b)** Mir tut der Finger weh. Heute ist es schlimmer als gestern.
   **c)** Meistens ist mir übel.

**Page 49**
1. **a)** I don't smoke. The risk is too great.
   **b)** Tobacco is totally unhealthy.
   **c)** A drug addict wastes his money.

2. **a)** Sie raucht zuviel.
   **b)** Drogen führen zu Kriminalität.
   **c)** Zigaretten riechen furchtbar.

**Page 51**
1. **a)** I'd like a sandwich with chips.
   **b)** Please bring me the menu.
   **c)** What is the dish of the day?
2. **a)** Ich möchte eine Flasche Limonade bitte.
   **b)** Bringen Sie mir bitte eine Packung Kekse.
   **c)** Eine Tasse Tee und eine Flasche Mineralwasser.

**Page 53**
1. **a)** I'd like to try the chocolates.

# Answers

## Lifestyle (cont.)

**b)** I had eaten breakfast at 7 o'clock.
**c)** We had gone to the standing café.
2. **a)** Er vermeidet Salz.
**b)** Es besteht aus Zucker und Fett.
**c)** Ich hatte das Steak probiert. Es war lecker!

**Page 55**
1. **a)** I never go into the grocery shop.
**b)** I'm looking for a new purse.
**c)** The price is too high!
2. **a)** Ich gehe oft ins Warenhaus.
**b)** Das Elektrogeschäft ist sehr gut.
**c)** Mein Bruder arbeitet in der Metzgerei / Fleischerei.

**Page 57**
1. **a)** I'm wearing a black skirt and an old pullover.
**b)** This dress suits you.
**c)** It is made of silk. It is wonderful.
2. **a)** Ich trage eine schwarze Hose und ein weißes Hemd.
**b)** Diese Stiefel sind zu klein.
**c)** Diese Jacke ist zu kurz.

**Practice Questions – Pages 58–59**
1. **für das Rauchen**: C and F; **gegen das Rauchen**: A, B, D, E, G and H
2. **a)** Dörte **b)** Jennifer **c)** Jennifer **d)** Patrick **e)** Dörte **f)** Patrick
**3. Example answers:**
**a)** Ich esse gern Schokolade und Pommes Frites. *I like eating chocolate and chips.* **b)** Ich rauche nicht. Ich find Rauchen total blöd. *I do not smoke. I think smoking is totally stupid.* **c)** Ich trinke selten Alkohol. Meine Eltern trinken auch nicht viel, weil es nicht gesund ist. *I rarely drink alcohol. My parents also do not drink much because it is not healthy.* **d)** Ich schwimme gern, ich spiele oft Badminton oder Tennis und ich esse viel Obst und Gemüse. *I swim a lot, I play badminton and tennis, and I eat a lot of fruit and vegetables.* **e)** Ich gehe nicht gern

einkaufen. *I do not like going shopping.* **f)** Ich trage gern eine Jeans und einen Pulli. Ich trage auch gern meine Mütze. *I like wearing jeans and a pullover. I also like wearing my hat.* **g)** Ich kaufe zum Beispiel Pralinen für meine Freundin, oder CDs für meinen Freund. *I buy, for example, chocolates for my (girl)friend or CDs for my (boy)friend.*

**4. Example answers:**
**a)** Um fit zu bleiben, gehe ich mindestens dreimal in der Woche schwimmen. Das ist gut für meine Gesundheit. *In order to keep fit I go swimming at least three times a week. That is good for my health.* **b)** Ich versuche, immer gesund zu essen. Ich esse jeden Tag Obst und Gemüse, aber ich mag auch Schokolade und Pommes! *I always try to eat healthily. I eat fruit and vegetables every day, but I also like chocolate and chips!* **c)** Meiner Meinung nach ist es sehr wichtig, fit und gesund zu bleiben. Wenn man nicht fit ist, kann man sehr leicht krank werden. *In my opinion it is very important to keep fit and healthy. If you are not fit you can become ill very easily.*

**5. Example answers:**
**a)** Am Samstag bin ich mit meiner Mutter einkaufen gegangen. Wir sind in viele Kleidergeschäfte gegangen. *On Saturday I went shopping with my mother. We went into lots of clothes shops.* **b)** Ich habe ein neues Kleid und eine gelbe Tasche gekauft. Meine Mutter hat Schuhe gekauft. Wir sind in ein Café gegangen. Ich habe Cola getrunken, und meine Mutter hat eine Tasse Kaffee getrunken. Wir haben beide ein großes Stück Schokoladentorte gegessen! *I bought a new dress and a yellow bag. My mother bought some shoes. We went to a café. I had a Coke and my mother had a cup of coffee. We both had a large piece of chocolate flan!* **c)** Ich verstehe mich gut mit meiner Mutter, und der Tag hat Spaß gemacht, aber wir haben nicht genug Zeit gehabt. Das nächste Mal werden wir das Haus früher verlassen, damit wir mehr Zeit fürs Einkaufen haben. *I get on well with my mother and the day was fun, but we didn't have enough time. Next time we will leave the house earlier so that we have more time for shopping.*

## Leisure and Free Time

**Quick Test – Page 61**
1. **a)** I sing in a choir.
**b)** I occasionally go to a concert.
**c)** I don't like watching love stories.
**d)** I'm not interested in classical music.
2. **a)** Ich sehe gern Horrorfilme und Abenteuerfilme.
**b)** Ich gehe nicht oft ins Kino.
**c)** Im Allgemeinen hören wir gern Popmusik und Rockmusik.
**d)** Ich habe die Nase voll von alten Science-Fiction Filmen.

**Page 63**
1. **a)** I've been playing the violin for one year.
**b)** Would you like to come to the rock concert at the weekend?
**c)** I play the guitar in order to relax.
2. **a)** Möchtest du ins Kino kommen? Ja. Toll!
**b)** Ich spiele seit fünf Jahren Schlagzeug.
**c)** Ich höre nicht gern klassische Musik. Es ist Blödsinn!

**Page 65**
1. **a)** At Christmas we get cards.
**b)** We have candles and we sing carols.
**c)** We decorate the Christmas tree.
2. **a)** Ich mag meinen Geburtstag feiern.
**b)** Wir sind im Dezember auf den Weihnachtsmarkt gegangen.
**c)** Ihre Verlobung war im Frühling.

**Page 67**
1. **a)** Handball is my favourite game.
**b)** I very much like to go walking in the hills.
**c)** I think water skiing is great!
2. **a)** Ich gehe sehr gern Windsurfen.

**b)** Gymnastik finde ich sehr interessant.
**c)** Wo ist der Spielplatz?

**Page 69**
1. **a)** I very much like to watch soaps.
**b)** My mother likes to watch sports programmes.
**c)** Our TV set doesn't work.
2. **a)** Kann ich die Sendung aufnehmen?
**b)** Ich sehe gern Musiksendungen.
**c)** Ich sehe nie die Nachrichten.

**Practice Questions – Pages 70–71**
1. **a)** Anna **b)** Manuel **c)** Ursula **d)** He hopes to get a tennis racquet (and he likes playing tennis) **e)** Manuel **f)** Science fiction books
2. **a)** Nora **b)** Ahmed **c)** Beate
**3. Example answers:**
**a)** Ich bleibe zu Hause. Meine Freundin kommt zu mir, und wir hören Musik, oder wir sehen fern. *I stay at home. My (girl)friend comes round and we listen to music or watch TV.* **b)** Ich bin mit meiner Familie an die Küste gefahren. Wir haben am Strand Fußball gespielt, aber, wir haben nicht im Meer geschwommen – es war zu kalt! *I went to the seaside with my family. We played football on the beach but we didn't swim in the sea – it was too cold!* **c)** Ich hoffe, mit meiner Familie in die Türkei zu fahren. *I hope to go to Turkey with my family.* **d)** Ich gehe nicht oft ins Kino – es ist zu teuer. Mein Lieblingsschauspieler ist Brad Pitt. *I don't often go to the cinema – it is too expensive. My favourite actor is Brad Pitt.*

**4. Example answers:**

**a)** Meine Geburtstagsparty war toll! Meine Tante, mein Onkel, mein Vetter und meine Kusine sind zu uns gekommen, und meine Eltern haben eine fantastische Mahlzeit vorbereitet. *My birthday party was great! My aunt, my uncle, and my cousins (male and female) came to our house, and my parents prepared a fantastic meal.* **b)** Ich habe CDs und Kleider bekommen, aber mein Lieblingsgeschenk war Geld, weil ich sehr gern einkaufen gehe. *I got CDs and clothes but my favourite present was money because I like going shopping.* **c)** Nächstes Jahr möchte ich meinen Geburtstag in Spanien feiern. Ich werde hundert Gäste einladen, und wir werden die ganze Nacht tanzen. *Next year I want to celebrate my birthday in Spain. I will invite a hundred guests and we will dance all night long.*

**5. Example answers:**

**a)** Wir hoffen an die Küste zu fahren. Wir werden mit dem Auto fahren. *We are hoping to go to the seaside. We will go by car.* **b)** Wir wollen am Strand in der Sonne liegen. Wir werden auch im Meer schwimmen, wenn es nicht zu kalt ist! Am Abend werden wir in einem Restaurant essen. *We want to lie on the beach in the sun. We will also go swimming in the sea, if it's not too cold! In the evening we will have a meal in a restaurant.* **c)** Das letzte Mal hat es geregnet. Wir sind im Auto geblieben, dann sind wir in ein Café gegangen, und haben eine Tasse Tee getrunken. Wir waren alle enttäuscht! *Last time it rained. We stayed in the car, then we went to a café and had a cup of tea. We were all disappointed!*

## Widening Horizons

**Quick Test – Page 73**

1. **a)** I very much like to go to Austria.
   **b)** Every year we go to Cologne.
   **c)** Normally we stay in the caravan.
2. **a)** Wir fahren mit dem Reisebus.
   **b)** Wir bleiben in einem Ferienhaus.
   **c)** München ist nicht am Meer / an der Küste.

**Page 75**

1. **a)** I was in Spain for three weeks.
   **b)** We had a tour of the town.
   **c)** The crossing was very good.
2. **a)** Wir sind eine Woche in Portugal geblieben.
   **b)** Ich fahre gern mit dem Schiff.
   **c)** Wo ist der Notausgang?

**Page 77**

1. **a)** A room for two people in the name of Schmidt.
   **b)** We would like to stay for three nights.
   **c)** We have no soap and the tap is not working.
2. **a)** Ich möchte vier Nächte bleiben.
   **b)** Ein Zimmer mit einem Blick auf die Berge.
   **c)** Ich habe meine Sonnenbrille verloren.

**Page 79**

1. **a)** It is thundering and lightning.
   **b)** It will be hot later.
   **c)** In the morning it will be sunny.
2. **a)** Es regnet und es ist kalt.
   **b)** Die Wettervorhersage für Donnerstag ist gut.
   **c)** Heute ist es wolkig und bedeckt.

**Page 81**

1. **a)** In the town centre there is too much traffic.
   **b)** We should be concerned about the environment.
   **c)** This district is calm and clean.
2. **a)** Wir recyceln Glas und Papier.
   **b)** Wir müssen die Umwelt schützen.
   **c)** Meine Stadt ist nicht sehr sauber.

**Page 83**

1. **a)** The greenhouse effect is a big problem for us all.
   **b)** We must protect the animals.
   **c)** We use too much carbon gas.
2. **a)** Ich kümmere mich um die Verschmutzung.
   **b)** Wir gebrauchen zu viele Spraydosen.
   **c)** Die ultravioletten Strahlen sind gefährlich.

**Page 85**

1. **a)** People eat this dish in the evening.
   **b)** I find the differences fascinating.
   **c)** When you are in Britain you normally have to queue.
   **d)** The specialty of the region is very sweet.
2. **a)** Es besteht aus Fisch. Es ist sehr gewürzt.
   **b)** Man isst es mit Brot.
   **c)** Dieses Gericht ist sehr mild.

**Practice Questions – Pages 86-87**

1. **a)** E **b)** D **c)** B **d)** F **e)** C **f)** A
2. **a)** Switzerland **b)** For a skiing holiday. **c)** Ten days. **d)** By coach.
   **e)** It was long and tiring. **f)** A holiday apartment. **g)** Very cold and there was snow. **h)** Played chess.

**3. Example answers:**

**a)** Ich gehe sehr gern mit meiner Familie zelten. Mein Lieblingscampingplatz ist in Nordengland an der Küste. *I like to go camping with my family. My favourite campsite is in the north of England on the coast.* **b)** Letztes Jahr bin ich mit meiner Familie nach Spanien gefahren. *Last year I went to Spain with my family.* **c)** Ich habe viel geschwommen. Wir sind einkaufen gegangen, und wir haben in einem Restaurant gegessen. *I swam a lot, we went shopping, and we had a meal in a restaurant.* **d)** Das Wetter in Spanien war sehr heiß. *The weather in Spain was very hot.* **e)** Ich recycle Altpapier und Glas. Meine Familie hat nur ein kleines Auto. *I recycle waste paper and glass. My family has only a small car.*

**4. Example answers:**

**a)** Mein Lieblingsurlaub war in Nordengland auf dem Lande. Ich bin mit meiner Familie gefahren. Wir sind mit dem Auto gefahren. *My favourite holiday was in the north of England in the country. I went with my family. We went by car.* **b)** Wir sind in einem großen Ferienhaus geblieben. Wir haben lange Wanderungen gemacht. Das hat Spaß gemacht, weil die Landschaft sehr schön war. *We stayed in a large holiday cottage. We had long walks. It was fun because the scenery was very beautiful.* **c)** Nächstes Jahr möchte ich nach Schottland fahren. Ich habe gehört, dass die Leute sehr freundlich sind, und die historischen Sehenswürdigkeiten sollten auch interessant sein. *Next year I would like to go to Scotland. I have heard that the people are very friendly, and the historic sights are also supposed to be interesting.*

**5. Example answers:**

**a)** In meiner Stadt gibt es zu viel Verkehr. Abgase verschmutzen die Luft, und es gibt auch viele Staus. *In my town there is too much traffic. Exhaust fumes pollute the air and there are also lots of traffic jams.* **b)** Man sollte Autos vom Stadtzentrum total verbieten. Ich würde auch mehr Fußgängerzonen haben. Wir sollten das Auto weniger benutzen, und mehr zu Fuß gehen. *They should ban cars entirely from the town centre. I would also have more pedestrian areas. We should use the car less and walk more.* **c)** Es ist sehr wichtig, sich um die Umwelt zu kümmern. Wir müssen die Erde schützen, sonst machen wir große Probleme für unsere Kinder. *It is very important to care about the environment. We must protect the earth, otherwise we create great problems for our children.*

# Index